9 —

D0556877

AN EVOLUTIONARY APPROACH
TO JESUS OF NAZARETH

JESUS OF NAZARETH YESTERDAY AND TODAY

AN EVOLUTIONARY APPROACH TO JESUS OF NAZARETH

JUAN LUIS SEGUNDO

*Edited and translated from the Spanish
by John Drury*

ORBIS BOOKS

Maryknoll, New York 10545

The Catholic Foreign Mission Society of America (Maryknoll) recruits and trains people for overseas missionary service. Through Orbis Books Maryknoll aims to foster the international dialogue that is essential to mission. The books published, however, reflect the opinions of their authors and are not meant to represent the official position of the society.

Originally published as *Lineas actuales de interpretación de Jesús de Nazaret,* which is Part 4 of Volume II of *El hombre de hoy ante Jesús de Nazaret,* copyright © 1982 by Ediciones Cristiandad, S.L., Huesca, 30–32, Madrid, Spain

English translation © 1988 by Orbis Books
Published in the United States of America by Orbis Books, Maryknoll, NY 10545
Manufactured in the United States of America

LIBRARY OF CONGRESS
Library of Congress Cataloging-in-Publication Data

Segundo, Juan Luis.
    [Lineas actuales de interpretación de Jesús de Nararet. English]
    An evolutionary approach to Jesus of Nazareth / Juan Luis Segundo:
edited and translated from the Spanish by John Drury.
        p.   cm. — (Jesus of Nazareth, yesterday and today: v. 5)
    Translation of: Lineas actuales de interpretación de Jesús de
Nazaret.
    Bibliography: p.
    Includes index.
    ISBN 0-88344-588-3 (pbk.)
    1. Jesus Christ—Person and offices.   2. Evolution—Religious
aspects—Christianity.   I. Drury, John, 1936-   .   II. Title.
III. Series: Segundo, Juan Luis.   Hombre de hoy ante Jesus de
Nazaret.   English; v. 5.
BT205.S45613 1988
232—dc19   88-4867
                                                         CIP

Somewhere in this world there exists a group, a community of persons, with whom I discussed the themes of these volumes one night a week for almost twenty years. We, the members of that group, became more than friends. We became brothers and sisters. By now it is almost impossible for me to say which thoughts are my own and which I owe to others in the group.

Participating in that group were people who became Christians only in adulthood, who were not yet Christians when we were talking about the topics that fill these volumes. But all of us were equally captivated by Jesus of Nazareth, and the quest for him made us even more brotherly and sisterly.

Some members of that community are now far removed in space, though not in affection. Others became part of that reflection and affection at a later date. To all of them I dedicate these volumes, not as a personal gift from me but as a duty honored: a work returned to those who brought it to life.

JUAN LUIS SEGUNDO

Contents

INTRODUCTION

A Jesus for Today

"Every human being and every generation has to experience, discover, and put together its own gospel about Jesus,"[1] if for no other reason than to salvage one of the great treasures that the past offers us vis-à-vis the problem of human existence and its meaningfulness.

But this is no arbitrary task in the case of Jesus, as it would not be in the case of any other figure. It is no easy matter to specify the *present-day* significance of any historical personage, whether we focus on specific aspects of the person or the person's overall life.

The *present-day* significance of someone who lived in a past age must entail two objective components: (1) the historical data on that person we possess; (2) the real-life problems faced here and now by an individual, a group, a society, or perhaps even humanity in general whether it knows it for sure or not.

In the preceding volumes we have seen both elements at work. Obviously one or the other can crumble a bit. Obviously any synthesis or bridge between the two can weaken at some point in time. That is why we must keep creating christologies day after day. That is why we must keep interpreting the great figures of history day after day.

My intention in Volume V is not so much to build *one* bridge between Jesus of Nazareth and today's human being. Rather, it is to point up some of the preconditions entailed in any effort to relate and convey the significance of that historical figure to present-day humanity. So I should like to begin by dealing with two possible misunderstandings on the part of people who would agree in principle with my formulation of the issue. These misunderstandings stem from the fact that they do not pose the matter in all its depth and complexity, or do not draw all the consequences that must be drawn, in my opinion, if the synthesis is to be truly alive and effectively meaningful. Note that I say nothing about the synthesis being 'perennial'.

I

The first misunderstanding is the assumption that we already possess one of the elements required for historical fidelity to Jesus of Nazareth, so all our

1

attention and creativity should be focused on the other element. In other words, the assumption is that we already possess all that we really need to know about the history of Jesus of Nazareth, so our problem is to make him speak our language today and truly address our problems.

Before I explain why this misunderstanding is a fatal obstacle to any effort to give present-day significance to historical figures of the past, let me verify its actual existence as a problem on various levels.

I will begin with the level of scholarly or scientific exegesis. We find, paradoxically enough, that the two most widely known opposing opinions tend to agree that the historical quest for Jesus of Nazareth is pretty much over. To explain this fact, we must go back a bit in time.

As we saw in Volume II, the documents most akin to a 'history' of Jesus are the Synoptic Gospels; yet their authors were aware of the fact that they were writing 'christologies' rather than histories. They felt that they had the right to inject into their narrative account of the events surrounding Jesus the understanding about him that they had gained in the light of his death, his resurrection, the actual life of the ecclesial community, and faith.

We must assume that this creative awareness was present in other New Testament authors, who were more blatantly theological or 'christological'. Such would be the case with Paul and John, for example, even though the author of the fourth Gospel goes back to the narrative genre and introduces valuable historical and geographical data.[2]

Now this basic awareness, this historical 'prudence', was lost fairly soon in the history of Christianity. We find two indications of this fact outside the New Testament, and even in the New Testament itself we can detect a tendency in the same direction. The first indication is the rise of 'apocryphal' gospels attributed to various apostles. The second indication is the tendency to make *one* gospel out of the four, as exemplified in Tatian's *Diatessaron*.

Insofar as the 'apocryphal gospels' are concerned, the main reason why the Church rejected them seems clear enough. It was not so much that all their data were false, but that the Church felt they were a byproduct of curiosity rather than a product of faith. An informative example here is the genre of 'infancy narratives' in Matthew and Luke, which underwent lavish growth in many apocryphal works. In an earlier volume I presented good reasons why this genre must be viewed as 'theological', and clearly so, even though at first glance the infancy narratives do not seem to be that different from the rest of the gospel narratives about Jesus' public life and ministry. Matthew and Luke use the infancy narratives to situate their readers within a framework of Old Testament messianic traditions that will better help them to understand the later activity and message of Jesus. The evangelists report the latter in a much more 'historical' way, even though postpaschal interpretation does play a role in their presentation of events. Logically then, and probably in fact as well, the infancy narratives must be considered the *last* part of the Synoptic Gospels to be written. In them we can see surfacing something of the literary genre that will be used by the author of John's Gospel.

Thus the *messianic* understanding of the child Jesus is framed in terms that will prepare readers to enter more easily into the narratives about his ministry. Jesus is the new Moses, spared in Egypt from the slaughter of the holy innocents. Jesus is the descendant of David, destined to restore his kingdom: born of a virgin and in Bethlehem because of his Davidic genealogy. Perhaps he is also the Servant of Yahweh, destined to suffering and death that will redeem Israel.

Over against the clearcut theological intention of the infancy narratives we have the narrative sobriety of the Synoptic Gospels with regard to the first thirty years of Jesus' life before his public ministry. This attracted the attention of people who became fascinated with Jesus after the paschal events, and who wanted at all costs to have more 'information' about him. The apocryphal narratives were an attempt to fill the gap.

It is certainly true that the *content* of the Synoptics intermixes history and theology. But the line of demarcation between them, which certainly must have been clear to the authors or editors, lies in various indications of a change in literary genre that we can detect. The apocryphal gospels, by contrast, attempt to fill in the gap between the two areas and their corresponding literary genres. The added narratives of the apocryphal gospels clearly indicate that awareness of the difference in content and genre is being lost.

The *Diatessaron* of Tatian is a second example and indication of this same loss of awareness. As I have just noted, people did not notice the difference in literary genres existing even in the Synoptics when they equated the content of the infancy narratives with the rest of those gospels. But even insofar as the rest of the gospel narratives are concerned, which are much more historical, we find a parallel difference between the Synoptics and John. To *intermix* Johannine data with the Synoptic data, as the *Diatessaron* does, is to produce an irreparable confusion of literary genres and much historical damage insofar as the life of Jesus is concerned.[3]

Moreover, there are fairly significant differences in the Synoptics regarding Jesus' public ministry. And one of the most important *historical criteria* for exploring these differences is the perception of the different christologies that distinguish the three Synoptic evangelists from one another: Matthew from Luke, in particular.

To give just one major example: How are we to arrive at the most historically reliable version of the beatitudes, if we are not aware at the start of the different focuses of 'theological' attention held by the two evangelists who cite them in such different form?

Readers of Volume II can readily imagine the obstacles to any such undertaking. If one prefers Luke's version, will one therefore omit the beatitudes addressed to the meek, the merciful, the peace-makers, and the pure of heart that appear only in Matthew? Not to mention the fact that such a choice eliminates the beatitude for none other than the 'poor in spirit' (with its touch of comfort for those who are materially rich) and 'those who hunger and thirst for justice'.

The tendency not to bypass anything said by Jesus could lead to the opposite solution. One would choose Matthew's version of the beatitudes, which *literally* includes everything that Luke has. But then what about the following "woes" that only Luke has. They stand out in sharp antithesis, and they are addressed by Jesus to the rich (not 'of spirit' either), the satisfied, and those who are laughing now.

In any case, it should be obvious that the worst possible solution would be to intermingle here the social situations of which Luke is speaking and the moral virtues of which Matthew is speaking, pretending that both reproduced the thinking of Jesus himself. No less important is the fact that one's option regarding the beatitudes will decide how one ends the parable of the banquet. Does one include the final scrutiny of the guests and whether they are wearing a wedding garment or not? The fact is that this ending is compatible only with the theology of Matthew. It makes no sense at all if one chooses Luke's version of the beatitudes.

There was no little opposition to the generalized use of the *Diatessaron*. We may assume that this opposition and canonization of the *three* Synoptic Gospels (rather than just one of them) stemmed from some sort of awareness that it was important to read the Gospels separately if one wanted to find the indispensable historical basis in the various interpetations of Jesus of Nazareth.[4]

What importance should we attach to these two indications of a gradually diminishing awareness that the documents on Jesus are a mixture of historical data and theological interpretations based on faith? Specifying the exact degree of importance is really little more than a properly academic question because the fact is that for many centuries the problem of the historical Jesus, as it has been called for the last century, was not considered an issue.

More than once in these volumes, and particularly in Volume IV where I offered Ignatius's *Spiritual Exercises* as a striking example, I made the point that this lack of attention to the historical density and complexity of Jesus' historical life was due to the ever-growing primacy of top-heavy 'christologies from above'. *Once God became the starting point* for explaining the existence of Jesus as the earthly existence of a divine being, of the Son of God, the relevance of his real-life history was reduced to two basic points, one negative and the other positive. The negative point was being able to show that *nothing* in the accounts of his life contradicted his status as Son of God.[5] The positive point, which seemed to suffice for *all* christological formulations of crucial importance to humanity, was the singular *historical* fact that Jesus had been killed for human beings despite his innocence.[6]

It was not that the rest of Jesus' life held no interest or value. As we saw in Volume IV, it was used to provide pious examples and moral lessons. But its incomparable value lay in its divine source, in the fact that its source was the one and only human being who participated in God's very nature.[7] When the Gospels offered two different versions of a particular item in Jesus' historical life, one was free to choose the one that seemed more suitable and appropriate. The only proviso was that the chosen alternative did not undermine anything that seemed proper to his divine nature, as compared with the other alternative. We can see the process at work with regard to the disconcerting finale of his life on the cross. Christians felt it necessary to complement the versions of Mark (15:34) and Matthew (27:46) with the version provided by Luke (23:42, and especially 23:46).

I shall not dwell further on this matter. Here my intention is to compare the outcome of the above approach with the outcome of the approach that sought to reconsider the problem of the *historical Jesus* in more scholarly, scientific terms.

Strange as it may seem, it was not theology proper that initiated this return to the sources. The origin of this movement must be sought in the wide-ranging cultural effort of the Enlightenment to bring everything instinctive, emotional, and irrational in human beings before the bar of reason.

From the Renaissance on, we find traces of this basic movement to rationalize the 'Jesus mystery', and to start by digging up his true 'history'. But these isolated efforts became focused and systematized in the eighteenth and nineteenth centuries. By now the two extreme viewpoints have been pretty well put in their place: that Jesus never existed; that we know every possible thing we need to know about his history. Yet the outcome is strange and paradoxical. We find two opposite tendencies that seem to arrive at the same *theological* consequences. One tendency is represented by Rudolf Bultmann, the other by Joachim Jeremias.

Both would probably agree that in the last two or three centuries all the major techniques of science and scholarship have been applied to the documents dealing with the history of Jesus. There agreement would end, however. Bultmann would maintain that we cannot know anything certain about Jesus of Nazareth, except such general things as the fact of his existence and his death on the cross. On that position he would build his own theological hypothesis, maintaining that the quest for a reliable history of Jesus is a wrong road leading nowhere.[8] Instead of looking for his 'history' in the biblical documents, we should let ourselves be summoned and challenged by the paradigmatic figure of those documents. Only then will we discover the true meaning of Jesus, for us today as for human beings in the past.

Although he does not formulate a theological theory in his exegesis, Joachim Jeremias would seem to stand poles apart from Bultmann. Certainly that would seem to be the case with respect to our chances of acquiring correct or fairly reliable data about the period of Jesus' public ministry and his death on the cross. Jeremias and many contemporary exegetes would suggest that we are in a strange position today. Because of the progress of historical and exegetical disciplines (our present-day knowledge of oriental languages, for example), we in the twentieth century are really much closer to the real Jesus than were people living in the fifth century.

It is certainly true that we have come to know all sorts of data relating to the historical Jesus, thanks to studies and excavations over the past few centuries. One example, embodied in Jeremias and his exegesis, is our greater knowledge of the language used by Jesus himself and the language used by the gospel writers. We also know much more about the economic, social, and political context of Jesus' life and message and of those who formulated interpretations of him in the Gospels and other writings. All these things shed much light on the history of Jesus' life and message. The intelligent use of this data, applied for example to Jesus' parables, presents us with something that is historically more coherent, original, and trustworthy.

Whether or not we have gotten our fill of reasonably certain data about Jesus of Nazareth, we do have the impression that nothing of *crucial* importance will be added in the near future. A prudently reconstructed 'historical Jesus' is the solid base that christologies should offer Christian faith today.

But a surprise awaits us. The conclusions often drawn from this modern confidence in approaching the life of Jesus tend to converge with those drawn by Bultmann from his very different position. Why?

Even with the data we possess, we cannot construct a 'biography' of Jesus as the basis of our faith in him. Guerrero explains: "Because any biography must fit its subject into some sort of type or scheme—prophet, philosopher, socioreligious leader, priest, wandering preacher—and the life of Jesus cannot be fitted into any such frame." Guerrero cites W. Trilling: "In Jesus the types useful in other cases do not work, and the clearcut motives to be found in the behavior of any human being are not present."[9]

I do not intend to delve into the problem just raised, but with the aid of our earlier analysis I would like to offer two observations that seem relevant here.

My *first* observation has to do with assertions made by Guerrero and Trilling. If it were true that Jesus and his historical base cannot be reduced or fitted into any interpretive types or categories, then he would not offer any basis whatsoever for either anthropological or religious faith. Only a meaningful unity or whole, a type of human being, can inspire a faith. As we saw in Volume I, the mainspring of faith is the search for a privileged witness to some *concrete* path leading to human fulfillment and happiness. If no key opens the the basic historical data we possess about Jesus of Nazareth, if indeed "the clearcut motives to be found in the behavior of any human being are not present,"[10] how could faith develop in something so devoid of meaning and sense?

Guerrero cites E. Trocmé to the effect that each person must try for an 'intuitive grab' at Jesus.[11] This makes perfect sense if we are indeed faced with a 'historical mystery'. But that takes us back by the opposite road to the very point in Bultmann's interpretation that has been widely criticized: i.e., the lack of a criterion, based on the historical Jesus, that might pass objective judgment on the fidelity of various christological interpretations. Here we have the paradoxical convergence of the two extreme positions.

II

My *second* observation entails points that require treatment in a section of their own. It has to do with the commonplace mistake made about what we might call objective historical knowledge.

Some events in history might be considered "pinpoint" events that are fairly sharply defined: e.g., How and when did Caesar cross the Rubicon? To determine the facts, I will rely more on a person who presents 'objective' documentary proof than on some enthusiastic partisan who is inclined to clothe Caesar in all the virtues and triumphs imaginable.

My situation is very different, however, when I am looking at a complicated historical reality, on which there is an abundance of anecdotal material, the *meaning* of which I am trying to grasp in some unified way because I somehow sense that it may have important elements of meaningfulness for today. It may be the whole trajectory of a person like Julius Caesar, of an institution like the Roman Empire, or of a certain period of history such as that of the barbarian invasions.

Of course I am talking here about serious, scientific, objective history. I am not talking about using some historical event, verifiable or not, to communicate with the timeless symbol of one or more crucial elements in human existence. I am not suggesting that such communication holds no interest for us. Bultmann is right in regarding Paul as a particularly paradigmatic example of such an approach. The point is that we, like Paul, want such communication to be more than a mere projection of subjective and perhaps distorted needs. Though our present context may be different and novel, we want our communication to be faithful to the *history* of the person, institution, or epoch in question.[12]

To correct or balance the mistaken notion under consideration here, I would state the following principle: *historical comprehension* of a more scientific and objective sort requires that we start with some interpretive scheme, originating in the present with which we are involved, and retroject it from our situation today back into the past. The apparent 'neutrality' of the historical observer serves only to strew the road with historical 'mysteries' which *seem* to be scientific, but which in fact are helpless in the face of the most varied and subjective interests rushing in from the present. Thus the Jesus who presents 'surprising contradictions', or who transcends any and all alternatives, proves to be the most helpless Jesus in the face of the most blatant ideological manipulations.[13] Paradoxically enough, that Jesus is the least historical Jesus and the most insecure basis for faith.[14]

The fact is, and experience proves it, that the mere accumulation of reliable historical data about Jesus is not enough to guarantee his significance. Something else is needed as well. It will not come from launching intellectual nets, neutral schemas, and disengaged hypotheses back into the past. Perhaps here more than anywhere else the words that Augustine has God address to the human being prove to be concrete and to the point: "You would not be seeking me, if you had not already found me." What is needed is a commitment here and now, *but not any sort of commitment or one that can be calculated in advance*. It is that commitment, *that wager*, that is capable of restoring Jesus of Nazareth to us from the past: alive and meaningful.

But when we adopt this approach and manage to fit the scattered historical pieces into a coherent whole, we find that the past sends us back again to our own conflict-ridden situation today. The historical Jesus confronts us once again with the problem of our own *ideologies*, the very problem we foolishly thought we could solve through our *faith*. We have faith in a historical figure, you see, who had to try to flesh out certain human values with a system of means rooted in, and limited by, a context that was likewise limited. Hence those means are not transferable; they cannot be slavishly copied, or used directly as such to measure our reality today. And of course our reality is not one for all human beings.

It is important, however, to note the precise meaning of the expression, 'today's human being', when used in connection with the hermeneutic wager I have in mind.

The label *fundamentalism* is used when people do not take into account the temporal dimension that necessarily intervenes between the comprehension of some figure from the past and our present-day situation. It is closely associated with ideology in the negative sense: i.e., something characterized by passive ignorance of the factors that condition our cognition. We think our knowledge is spontaneous, concrete, and well informed when in fact it is manipulated and alienated.

As is the case with ideology, most people say they are against fundamentalism, which is said to be naïve and infantile. Its dangerous nature is waved aside, as is that of practically all popular phenomena that find shelter under the cloak of religion. But that does not stop its diffusion on the mass level or affect its ideological importance as a social phenomenon.

Even more important here is another fact. As is the case with ideology, people think they can get around fundamentalism with mere declarations. These declarations admit in principle that there must be mediations between Jesus and us. But this admission is so rudimentary in nature that all sorts of loopholes are left open for more subtle forms of fundamentalism.

Speaking very generally, people grant that we must speak to today's human being in categories that make Jesus comprehensible and meaningful. But the criteria used to determine those categories are more subjective than objective.[15] What would be meaningful for today's human beings? What they, as opposed to the people of Jesus' day, would be able to accept.

Bultmann's case for demythologization is a typical example. Today's humanity is the product of the Enlightenment, accustomed to science and technology. It can hardly accept the mythical conceptions that were held so readily by people almost two thousand years ago. That would apply, among other things, to all that the Bible presents as miraculous, as due to direct divine intervention and suspension of the laws of nature.

Without going into that specific issue here, I must say that many of these efforts to build a bridge of meaningfulness between Jesus of Nazareth and our time suffer from a lack of critical-mindedness. Hence they prove to be false escapes from the temptation of fundamentalism. They are too quick to erase the necessary boundaries between the objective problematic of today's human beings (who are geographically, culturally, and socially situated) and their own efforts to make the meaning of Jesus easy and painless.

Thus many christological efforts fall into reductionism, under the pretext of adaptation. Take the antagonism and conflict aroused and heightened by Jesus of Nazareth. Besides posing a difficulty to the official Churches, who are inclined to pay any price to ensure their quantitative universality, the conflictive aspect of Jesus is exorcised on the grounds that it shocks today's human being. As if it did not profoundly shock human beings of his own day! Remember that Paul had to make difficult and necessary adaptations in his time. Even he may momentarily have succumbed to the temptation to get Jesus across to people of Greek culture without being shocking or strident. At least that is the impression we may get when we compare his discourse in Athens (Acts 17:22f.) with his analysis of pagan enslavement to Sin in Romans 1.

The point here is that we must be careful when we describe today's human being as one who is rational, scientific, pragmatic, mature, and radically secular; or even as one for whom 'God is dead'. We must distinguish two very different things.

On the one hand it is certainly true that unnecessary shocks should be avoided. Jesus himself, for example, made it clear that his 'miracles' were not meant to *prove* in a verifiable way that God was with him, violating the most obvious natural laws. Parapsychology is not new. Even if we adopt the characteristically modern view that Jesus merely enjoyed special talent as a healer, his own primary sense of those deeds remains intact. He saw them as signs of the nearness of God's kingdom, which was coming in power to benefit the poor and the marginalized.

On the other hand we cannot bow to every definition or demand of the 'modern' human being. If being scientific or pragmatic means illogically or irrationally refusing to allow for any datum that transcends empirical verifiability, then any adaptation to that mentality will necessarily reduce the life and message of Jesus to mere fable. It will call nothing into question because it will mean nothing. Not because there is nothing to question, but because we are faced with an *a priori* obtuseness and close-mindedness to any criterion that shakes up the prevailing *superficial* consensus. In the name of today's culture people uncritically accept the established view, only because that is the easiest thing to do.

To sum up, then, we can never be completely objective in our reconstruction of the past; but such reconstruction is necessary to bring some personage of history into our own present. That holds true for Jesus of Nazareth too.

However, there are ways of getting closer to objectivity that will help us to rule out the more pernicious kinds of subjective criteria.

III

Volume V of this work does not claim to erect a christology for today's human being. I could not do so, for the reasons already spelled out in the previous sections of this chapter.

It could not do so for another reason that I have been harping on from the very beginning. Understanding Jesus of Nazareth as someone who is meaningful for present-day humanity cannot be the result of an intellectual effort. It is not a theoretical science or a logical tract; it is a practical art.

If we must keep using the term 'christology', it can only mean the ongoing work of the community to deal with the objective problems of some area of today's world by trying to introduce elements of the anthropological or religious faith of Jesus of Nazareth into the solutions for those problems. We will not do this because we opt for some magical form of belief, but because we have experienced the human expansiveness and enrichment provided by that faith; and we therefore assume that the same will continue to be true so long as we creatively relate it to the real-life problems facing humanity.

In that sense my whole effort in these volumes, and particularly here in Volume V, can be described as a methodical acceptance of the challenge embodied in Guerrero's apt and profound observation: "We would save ourselves much wasted effort to gain believers *in* Jesus if instead we tried to interest human beings in what was truly original in Jesus' life—his faith, i.e., the faith *of* Jesus."[16] Needless to say, this shift of interest from faith *in* Jesus to the faith *of* Jesus does not exempt us from the inescapable task of translating it into present-day categories.

The only thing I can do here is sketch some of the objective formulations of problems that I believe to be radically new and that must be faced by any humanism. In an equally sketchy way I will then try to show which elements in the 'faith of Jesus' can enrich our posing of those problems. A brief enumeration of the issues should make it easier for my readers to feel at home with the remaining chapters of this volume.

(1). Until the last fifty years or so, human beings were not, and could not be, consciously aware of the active, creative role that is properly and inevitably theirs in the continuation of universal or biological evolution. At the very least they cannot avoid that role within the limited confines of our own planet.

The notion that the universe has undergone evolution, and that *homo* is the most conscious product of that process, is more than a century old; the diffusion and victory of its scientific version is far from uniform, of course. But even when restricted to the biosphere (i.e., to the biological evolution of life), the idea of evolution has posed serious problems for the Christian conception of the world and the human being. The proof is that at first it was violently rejected as being contrary to dogma; and specifically to dogmas closely bound up with the significance of Jesus, such as the dogmas of original sin and redemption.

There was also a vague feeling that all the categories used to express the meaning of Christ for us had been *fixist*, from those of the New Testament on. They had been independent of, and probably opposed to, any evolutionary hypothesis. Confronting this hypothesis, even in the sacred books of the Bible, was a frightening challenge if it in fact meant that everything would have to be reformulated in categories that were definitely not biblical.

The discovery of the earth's revolution around the sun had provoked serious problems because such a view seemed incompatible with a few biblical passages of secondary importance. Readers can well imagine, then, what it meant to situate the whole content of the Bible, and particularly God's 'definitive' revelation in Jesus, within the context of a hypothesis shaped by human beings. And this remained true even when people sensed that the final result might have more coherence and plausibility.

Until the last fifty years or so, as I noted above, evolution remained little more than a scientific hypothesis or thesis. Then two factors entered the picture that had not been encountered since the world began. The first factor was humanity's newly acquired capacity to annihilate life on our planet in a quick, irreversible way. The second factor, dovetailing with the first and accentuating its importance, was the possibility of annihilating life on our planet more gradually yet relatively soon. But in this case there would be no deliberate decision. It would come about in an easier way: by our lack of decision. That is precisely what we see today in our reckless and unbridled use of nature's resources.

Note that this is not the largely *subjective* question as to what today's human beings can or cannot accept in the Bible, the New Testament, and the literary genres they use. We are facing an *objective* problem that could never have been posed so urgently and radically before, and that cannot be avoided now. Given the relative silence of even the Churches, we logically find ourselves asking whether Jesus of Nazareth still has any valid significance in the face of these issues. And if he does, what is it exactly?

The recent appearance of new and awesome problems should not prompt us to give a negative answer right away. The theory of evolution, which first appeared as a scientific hypothesis, has come a long way. It had to overcome much oversimplification, arbitrariness, and prejudice before it could become a task for us. Today, however, we are faced with the challenge of *managing* or steering evolution on our planet. We must consciously and deliberately take the reins of evolution, if we wish to avoid fatal mistakes; but it is no easy task. We possess awesome means and resources, but we know little about managing them. Thus the challenge facing us implies, to some extent, a return to the past: not just to the recent past but to the remote past. We must return to the past to discover the *mechanisms* of the evolution that we are undergoing, and that we must somehow imitate in order to survive. We are sailing in treacherous waters, and we clearly need a good sea chart if we are to avoid shipwreck.

Now when we have talked about the creative task of framing the significance of Jesus of Nazareth in a given historical context, we have been in the habit of viewing historical contexts and cultures as relatively independent organic entities. Toynbee, for example, depicts earlier cultures as organisms arising, growing, and dying, to be replaced by *other* cultures. That may have been relatively true in the past, but with our present-day civilization or culture we have entered a *universal* context. It is not that everything has become uniform, but that everything has become interrelated. Our present planetary context of culture will not be replaced by another, nor are there parallel alternatives to it. We cannot passively hope that some new and vigorous culture will replace our own exhausted one. No substitution is possible.

We cannot simply 'acculturate' the gospel message to 'today's human being' as if we were dealing with one culture among many. For the first time in history, the Christian message and its function must somehow be pondered and lived in terms of the *mechanisms* of one sole and single evolutionary context.[17]

(2). The objectively *new* task facing us can be characterized by two adjectives that have never before been viewed in conjunction as they must now be. Our task is *ecological* and *political*.

In Volume I, we saw that ecology as a movement arose apart from politics in the usual sense of the term. The initial opposition between the two was quite natural. The ecological movement arose in the developed countries because they were the ones engaged in the maximum exploitation of natural resources; and that reckless policy still continues, destroying nature and its resources at an ever-increasing rate. Politics, and democratic politics specifically, gave free expression to the mad desire to possess more and more. To some extent this forced the representatives of the majority to keep expanding consumption without considering the price that had to be paid for it. Politics was, *par excellence*, the arena where one could not inculcate restraint. One could only respect and cater to the egotistical and catastrophic "interests" of the voting majority.

It is not surprising, therefore, that the ecological movement saw politicians as its natural adversaries. Hence the exodus to the political desert that marked the first phase of the ecological movement. Ecologists denounced the political ideologies used to justify the holocaust of nature, or else they turned indifferent to politics in general.

A change occurred when various ecological disasters became more visible and struck closer to home, threatening great numbers of people in the affluent nations. Ecology and politics now came together. Ecological slogans and parties arose, seeking to win more political power in order to reduce the excesses of suicidal consumption. Needless to say, these parties do not win the support of the masses insofar as they remain exclusively ecological; the masses are preoccupied with different problems that are more directly connected with political ideologies or strategies. But one development is interesting and noteworthy. For more or less self-interested reasons, traditional politics itself has become more attentive to ecological problems. More and more it has come to see the intimate relationship between ecology and politics.

When we look at the poor nations, on the other hand, we find that the separation of politics and ecology is almost a dogma of faith. Ecology is viewed as the selfish concern of the affluent nations, who are worried about preserving their own living space. This normally does not entail accepting radical changes in, or restrictions on, consumption; it simply means further exploitation of the less-developed nations in the system. Thus ecology is viewed as a betrayal of the authentic problems facing our poor countries.

There is no reason why this restricted, egotistical, and nationalistic view of ecology should prevail in our countries over a more radical and political one. Political analysis of the crucial phenomenon known as 'imperialism' is not new in our countries; it is sometimes referred to as 'dependence' to avoid the supposedly Marxist connotations of the other word. This analysis is, in fact, an ecological formulation of the issue in the fullest and best sense of the word. But since the ecological parties in the developed nations seem to be apolitical, at least when it comes to international relations between rich and poor countries, their ecology is regarded as an evasion in our countries. By the same token, our own analysis of imperialism or dependence in purely political terms often suffers from a lack of ecological categories, which translates into a loss of effectiveness.

One proof of this is the fact that our analysis is based primarily and preponderantly on a *quantitative comparision*. Some country or group of countries possesses more in terms of power or consumption. It is as if countries, like past cultures in Toynbee's treatment, were so many individual organisms of the same species: some more developed and powerful than others. Even Marxism, however universalist it may be in principle, arose before the appearance of the 'ecological' categories of the natural and economic sciences. Hence its use of dialectics tends to divide along *national* lines, as if one had to start over for each and every country.

None of the parties seems to have realized that the mere fact that one part of humanity has been forced to serve the consumption of the other part introduces an imbalance into the whole picture that will sooner or later destroy both. It is not just that the onslaught against nature continues in the 'dependent' countries in order to provide consumer goods at the lowest possible price, with the result that deserts continue to spread inexorably. Far more important is the resultant recklessness that can be seen and felt in human action and behavior—in sociopolitical behavior, to begin with.

The 'dependent' part of the world is forced to live with an ever smaller share of natural resources in absolute or relative terms. The logical response of people to these dramatic reductions is one of desperation. The worldwide reaction to this, in turn, is the toppling of a social order based on respect and support for initiative and freedom on both the individual and group level. As I write these words, we find all sorts of totalitarianism around us. Fifty-six countries in the United Nations, for example, are presently ruled by military juntas.

When we examine this fact in terms of ecological categories, we see clearly that democracy is not one political system to be chosen among many once the status of independent nation is reached. It is not a product of political 'intentionality' today, though it may have been in the past. Today it is a social equilibrium as fragile as the flora and fauna of a forest or the purity of river water.

It is depressing to see the naïveté of public-opinion papers in the underdeveloped countries, insofar as they present the democratic elections in the United States as an example we should imitate. They do not seem to notice that the *real* democracy of a country that consumes a terribly disproportionate share of the planet's resources constitutes an ecological catastrophe that makes democracy impossible, or constantly destabilizes it, in the countries that are supposed to imitate her example.[18]

Politics as a whole, then, must be considered in ecological terms. Or, to put it the other way, today any ecology seeking to protect the *whole* context necessary for a humane social life must be thought out in political terms, not only by those responsible for the imbalances but also by the victims. This politics, in turn, cannot focus on isolated organisms defined by political or national boundaries. It must focus on the great forces that surpass those boundaries, and that oblige all peoples to form a common circuit of mutual stimuli and responses.

We cannot find this ecological dimension in the exasperating political infantilism of the liberal center or right-of-center that exists in the underdeveloped nations. All we get are their cycles of authoritarian governments alternating, only in theory, with constitutionally established democratic institutions and some illusory guarantee of a national frontier.

The same lack of an ecological dimension is evident in the way the political left approaches its programs, whether in power or as an opposition force (the more usual case). It starts with the assumption that its programs can only center around the transition to socialism *in each individual country*. It goes without saying, of course, that today socialism is assumed to be the only real alternative to the prevailing capitalist system. The problem is that when these programs are conceived in a linear, non-ecological way, they entail increasingly higher human costs. The main one is a kind of *schizophrenia*, producing in the left incessant and innumerable political *schisms* (i.e., divisions). But how *concretely* are countries to move toward socialism when they belong to a multinational political bloc that rejects it, when they operate in an equally international market on which the socialist countries themselves depend either directly or as members of the rival bloc?

In countries that are not very wealthy or competitive, then, the policies of the political left fluctuate endlessly between two extremes, both of which are doomed in advance. On the one hand they settle for being 'socialisms of the future', operating right now in the context of present-day capitalism and its interests[19] because the international policy of present-day socialism demands it. Or else the fight for socialism becomes a continuing escalation of desperate means within local frontiers, leading to even more forceful oppression in return. In the first case the militant, waving the banner of revolution, is led to adopt an inconsistent and contradictory policy of reformism that has no direct connection with the creation of a socialist society. It leads merely to better incorporation into the capitalist system. The second alternative provokes further repression. Against all expectations, this repression can destroy the social ecology of the country without ever triggering the popular reaction that was expected to be crucial and decisive.

This is no minor or transitory problem. Neither is the matter of viewing politics and ecology together as two complementary dimensions that must be taken into account if we are to make existing society and human interrelationships more humane.

As we saw in Volume III, in his own specific context Paul spelled out the humanization of these relationships in terms of enslavement to Sin and liberation through Christ. Today we note the extraordinary and growing interdependence of all human beings on our planet. Does this have nothing to do with the significance of Jesus of Nazareth? Would his significance be crucial for human beings if it were not naturally—not just artificially—bound up with the major factors conditioning human survival as such on our planet?[20]

(3). The third issue is closely bound up with the first two issues. Evolution cannot take place by leaps. The main reason is an intrinsic one that we must try to incorporate into our whole way of thinking.

We have begun to perceive and appreciate a fundamental element in evolutionary mechanisms: *chance*. It intervenes as a crucial factor in both universal and biological evolution, whatever one's opinion may be about the presence or absence of *purpose* or finality in evolution. At every level evolution transforms by 'using' stochastic processes: i.e., chance subjected to the mathematical laws of probability.

Chance obviously can be put in the service of some purpose. In the strictest sense of the word a human being, for example, can 'use' stochastic processes (e.g., roulette) to supply himself or herself with money or emotions.

Now when compared with intrinsically purposive processes, stochastic processes are distinguished primarily by their slowness. A purposive process is one in which human beings themselves modify the causes of something in order to obtain a different effect. That difference could have been left to chance, which would have manifested it some day or other. A doctor, for example, will not use a stochastic process to cure a patient in great anxiety, pain, or danger. Using the more *rapid* principle of cause and effect, the doctor will diagnose the disease and prescribe the indicated medicine for combatting it. If any element of chance enters, it lies in the fact that the doctor may select *one* of a dozen or more indicated remedies and watch for any reactions or side-effects in the patient.

We know that the Lamarckian theory to explain evolution falls short because it does not take sufficient account of the role of chance. At first glance it would seem correct to say that if the *useful* characteristics acquired experientially by a species could then be transmitted by heredity, then evolution would have been much more rapid. But Lamarck formulated his theory before the science of genetics arose. That science proved the impossibility of transforming experientially acquired features into heredity, thereby confirming the paleontological data on the slowness of species variation. Much more importantly, it made clear that if stochastic processes had been replaced by purposive ones, irreversible catastrophes would have soon followed. In a situation where innumerable variables are operative, changing one or more of them in a sudden, drastic way will throw the whole complex out of balance. The 'useful' quality proves to be death-dealing, since it overloads circuits that are designed to solve problems through trial and error.

My readers will readily see the connection between these considerations and ecological thinking. Human beings may formulate specific proposals and try to incorporate them into some structure because they appear to be good in themselves. But the end result is ambivalent. The proposals solve one problem but create other problems.

Now it is clear that an irreversible change has taken place over the past twenty centuries of human existence. Ever-increasing communication and interdependence have broken down frontiers and *multiplied the variables* that must be taken into account in trying to implement some modification that is deemed advantageous. The Great Wall of China, for example, helped to keep China isolated for centuries, so that internal changes did not affect the outside world. Today, even if China were to remain relatively isolated, its population factor would still have a crucial effect on the world's political equilibrium.

The point of interest to us here is this: these realities have modified the relationship between *faith* and *ideologies* in an objective and decisive way. Otherwise, why do we feel so uneasy when we hear someone say: 'I am going to realize the kingdom of God on earth'? And why do we feel more uneasy insofar as the speaker possesses more power? Undoubtedly we feel that way because we are more or less aware of the complexity of the variables that make up our world. We almost instinctively think: How many individuals and groups will be crushed by this project? What will be the price of this 'internationality', which seems so just in principle? This one example should suggest that things which could be done when the world was composed of relatively watertight compartments become increasingly impossible or catastrophic today.

Some readers may object that this is not the case, since humanity has increasingly powerful means at its disposal. This means that humanity must be much more careful today in deciding what can or cannot be done than it had to be in the past.

Consider the situation in the first century when Jesus was alive. Clearly the relative isolation of Israel, even within the interdependence imposed by the Roman Empire, enabled Jesus to furnish his values, his *faith*, with a system of means that was his own. His system of means, or *ideology*, was original and unmistakable: i.e., his interpretation of the Law, the latter being recognized by Israel specifically as a norm and revelation deriving from God. Clearly Jesus' system of means was very primitive and enormously conditioned by the atypical socioreligious situation of Israel and its people.

There is no doubt that Jesus invested much creative originality in the means at his disposal, but their simplicity must be noted. Jesus could manage his set of instruments practically by himself. His disciples may have been important, especially later, but they do not seem to have had any crucial impact on his project during his lifetime. He did not need a team of specialists, nor did he use means that required a coalition of complex and intricate interests.

Jesus' effectiveness was rooted in his original and persuasive use of a means that was powerful in two ways: i.e., Scripture. It was powerful at that time and place in history because it represented something profoundly national for Israel. It was an anchor in the midst of the international waves that threatened to submerge Israel in total anonymity; and there was also an effervescence of apocalyptic, messianic, and Zealot tendencies at the time. It was also a powerful instrument because of the way Jesus used it. He interpreted it to liberate the poor and marginalized of Israel from their inhuman situation, thus gathering up a deep-rooted and visible human need of the majority and filling his sails with it.

Change that set of circumstances and Jesus' means no longer fill the bill. Paul himself found that out, not so many years after Jesus' death, when he tried to convey Jesus' message and its significance to areas that were more culturally integrated into the Roman Empire.

Let's pursue these reflections a bit further. Jesus had a profound impact on his people. Proof is the fact that his effectiveness system, after establishing a precarious balance of power, resulted in his political assassination. But if he did have an impact, the fact remains that he had only his *natural* adversaries. By that I mean that no one could compete with Jesus in attracting the people and getting their attention. No one else was around to cure lepers as he did. Moreover, there was no movie theater to go to, no television set at home, not even the 'bread and circuses' of the people in Rome. A lone voice could make itself heard in that silence, if it had something to say; and especially if it spoke in new, liberative accents of things that were profoundly national and sacred.

What would Jesus have done in the intercommunicating world of today? What price would he have had to pay to get his voice heard through the only media that ensure a wide audience? What Bible or what gospel message is today a living root, not just one book among many? Even granting that poor and marginalized people exist today as they did in his day, we might well ask what broadcast media would be at Jesus' disposal long enough for him simply to air his message and die?

I am not implying that in the realm of Christian meaningfulness, the faith *of* Jesus has no meaning or efficacy today. I am saying that the explosion of the old watertight compartments means that there is no way to formulate one specific system of means, one ideology, for transmitting that faith. The latter will continue to need ideologies as always, but it will be less and less able to label *one* single ideology as properly its own.

In short, Christian faith must accept the *slowness* of complex evolutionary processes and link up with quasi-stochastic procedures. A Christian politics

will not be one that builds 'Christian democracies'. Instead a truly Christian
politics may well adapt to different contexts, bear no specific label, and offer
that proper balance of various factors that will enable us to advance a few steps
toward democracy on a worldwide scale. Bateson rightly points out that no
quality is more important for the evolution of a species and its survival than
flexibility. So our question is: How can an interpretation faithful to the
concrete reality of Jesus of Nazareth prove itself to be a flexibility factor for the
human species?

IV

Answering this question requires special handling of the materials dealing
with Jesus of Nazareth. Right now my concern is with the New Testament
materials, so I would like to recall briefly a few points that have been made
elsewhere in these volumes.[21]

My approach here differs from that of Teilhard de Chardin. His christology
is largely of the Johannine type, it seems to me, undoubtedly because the
fourth Gospel goes furthest in transcending the time-bound categories in which
the real-life history of Jesus was inscribed. Using evolutionary categories, I
shall try to comprehend and explain the concrete, limited event that took place
once in human history: Jesus of Nazareth.

Readers might assume that we already have all the material we need for this
task, since we have examined the treatment of Jesus in the Synoptic Gospels
and Paul. Rejecting the notion of constructing *one* definitive, all-embracing
christology, we looked for the solid bedrock of reliable history about Jesus and
then saw how Paul creatively handled the task of interpreting Jesus for a
different historical context. Now all we need to do, it might seem, is to use the
data of the Synoptics in conjunction with objective data on the thought
categories that humanity must use today.

That is basically true. But it is also worth remembering that the canonical
New Testament presents a wide variety of interpretations of Jesus. This bur-
geoning of christologies from different viewpoints and contexts is not useless
repetition, nor is it merely an inducement to creativity. It means that an
enormous wealth of interpretation existed in written form, not too long after
Jesus' death, for the use of new generations of human beings who would place
their faith in him.

As I pointed out in earlier volumes, the data of these various christologies
cannot simply be *added* to one another. Presenting data from different viewpoints, they *multiply* our information; just as our various senses multiply the
sensations that become part of our *perception* of objects. In Volume III we saw
the process operative in Paul's treatment of Jesus. Although at one point Paul
indicates that Jesus died *for our sins* and was resurrected for our justification
(Rom 4:25), this interpretation is not to be confused with, or simply added to,
the historical cause of Jesus' death: his proclamation of the coming kingdom
and its conflict-ridden repercussions in the sociopolitical realm. We know Paul

himself did not do that. He clearly perceived the historical density of Jesus' project, showing us that its passage through death and resurrection is the key to understanding history and humanity's role in history.

I say all this because we are much inclined to use data from christologies 'from above' if we are attempting to frame the significance of Jesus in the perspectives of universal evolution. As I pointed out earlier, particularly in discussing the Council of Chalcedon (Volume IV, Chapter 1), christologies from above need not sacrifice the density of Jesus' history to metaphysical or religious speculations. There is that danger, but the proper balance can be maintained.

Not everything in Greek thought, much less in the Hebrew thought that pervades the *whole* New Testament, was static and fixist. The earliest christologies from above began to expand the significance of Jesus to the beginning and end of human time.[22] Paul saw Jesus as the *firstborn* of many brothers and sisters (Rom 8:29) and the new Adam (Rom 5:12; 1 Cor 15:22). Through him everything has its existence (1 Cor 8:6), and toward him all creation is striving as toward its full meaningfulness (Rom 8:29 f.) and liberation (1 Cor 15:24–28).[23] Yet Paul never lost the proper balance between christology from above and the historical project of the kingdom that framed Jesus' concrete life, even though it was a difficult task. Paul had to go through tortuous linguistic and conceptual routes to situate Jesus simultaneously in three temporal frames: past, present, and future. But every time he succeeded, I venture to say, we find ourselves with a harbinger of evolutionary language, the only language that can do justice to the universal dimensions of Jesus' *meaningfulness* without sacrificing his history.

Readers should note that in the following pages I do not feel obliged to explore Jesus' meaningfulness solely in terms of my study of the Synoptics and Paul in Volumes II and III. I will be guided by two negative criteria, however. I will not *mix* elements whose meaning is framed in, and derives from, different christologies.[24] Nor will I indulge in the *indiscriminate* use of christologies from above, to the point where we might forget the limited, concrete reality of Jesus' life and the definite key he chose to give it.

So I begin the modest but difficult task I have set for myself in this volume. I cannot help but recall what Julian Huxley wrote about interpreting human life in evolutionary terms, and I would like to paraphrase his words in terms of my present task: "Medieval theology obliged human beings to ponder the significance of Jesus of Nazareth *sub specie aeternitatis*, in the light of eternity. I am trying to rethink his significance *sub specie evolutionis*, in the light of evolution. I do so, I confess, with some trepidation."[25]

CHAPTER I

Toward a New Context

Trying to interpret the significance of Jesus of Nazareth some two thousand years ago, Paul found himself confronted with a strange question: Could creation—in lay terms, the universe—be subjected to uselessness in a permanent way? By itself could it be devoid of meaningfulness, unless humanity freely managed to give it meaning? Seventeen centuries later, Leibnitz asked himself whether the existing universe could or should be considered the best of all possible worlds.

Both Paul and Leibnitz felt they had data that helped to tip the scales in a given direction. Faced with the questions posed by the universe today, however, we vaguely perceive that our whole situation and problematic has changed, even if that fact does not in principle and logically exclude the problems of Paul and Leibnitz as utterly meaningless.

Something crucial has changed, to be sure. Looking back over the past, we cannot help but wonder if the old problems are those of humanity's childhood. Do they fall by the wayside now that the problems of adolescence and adulthood are upon us? Whatever the answer may be to that general problem, it is clear that *our context is new and different*. Even if we do confront the old problematic once again, we must do so from that new context and with different mental coordinates.

To depict this radical change and the reason behind it, Teilhard de Chardin uses a graphic image in one of his works:

Up to now human beings have been living at once dispersed and closed in on themselves, like passengers who have met by accident in the hold of a ship whose movement they did not even suspect. Living on the earth that brought them together in groups, they could find nothing better to do than to argue with each other or amuse themselves. Now, by chance, or better, by the normal effect of organization, our eyes have just opened. The most daring of us have mounted the bridge and seen the ship that has been carrying us all. They have glimpsed the foam produced by the prow as it cuts through the water. They have caught on to the fact that there is a boiler to be fed and a helm to be directed. Above all, they have seen the

21

clouds floating by and smelled the fragrance of the islands beyond the circle of the horizon. The agitation of the hold is no longer possible. Mere drifting is no longer possible. The time has come to pilot the ship. It is inevitable that a different humanity must emerge from this vision.[26]

Readers will undoubtedly share my own initial feeling that the image is brilliant and the conclusion persuasive. But I can't help but feel, upon reflection, that Teilhard de Chardin knew very well that a whole series of unanswered questions lay buried underneath his dazzling imagery. His concealment of these questions was not due to any lack of sincerity on his part, since he did treat them in other places. In this passage, however, he was anxious to drive home a particularly urgent point: after two or three million years of human life on earth we now, in this very generation, have reached a crucial point in that history. Up to now evolution has carried us along. We have been drifting as its outcome or result. With the help of various scholarly sciences, many of them no more than a century old, we can trace the broad course that the ship has followed while humanity argued or amused itself in the hold. But now we have discovered that we are on a ship and a voyage, that we must attend to the boiler and the helm. Thus everything has changed, or *should* have changed.

If we are realistic, you see, we must admit that we have noted only certain aspects of the change. A journey and a steering wheel at our disposal was a fantasy we nurtured in the hold with our science fiction; but it is often much harder for us to see the realism of it all when we are actually at the helm. We seem to be in the position of Phileas Fogg, the character of Jules Verne in *Around the World in Eighty Days*, stuck in a little wooden bark in the middle of the ocean and obsessed with the boiler of our ship. Combustible material on our planet seems to be running out. We do have the helm we had been dreaming of, but what use is it? To keep going, we must keep throwing all our wood in the boiler, sparing only enough to keep the ship afloat. Sooner or later, it seems, we will face a terrible option: either the boiler or the helm. For the helm, too, is made of wood.

Why is it that this image does not possess the optimism of Teilhard de Chardin's image, who was our contemporary after all? I think we would do well to analyze his image, commenting a bit on the realism of some elements in it as well as his deliberate or involuntary camouflaging of some latent problems.

I

One debatable element in his image here is something that did not escape Teilhard de Chardin himself in other places. The apparent break in continuity between the problems of the bridge (steering the ship) and the discussions in the hold is exaggerated and erroneous. And surely included in those latter discussions is the one that began two thousand years ago with Jesus of Nazareth and continues today.

Teilhard's image seems to suggest that human beings *wasted time* for centuries with their arguments and discussions in the hold of the ship. The content of those discussions apparently had little or nothing to do with what was really at stake: i.e., the destiny of the passengers. To what extent do history and prehistory have anything crucial to teach us about our 'now'? Is it possible that with the discovery of the bridge history had lost its position as the great 'teacher of life'? Have our problems today changed so radically that they owe nothing to the questions debated in earlier days?

This seeming discontinuity is underlined by three hypotheses, offered in Teilhard's image, as to what might have caused the transformation of our basic problematic: (1) the 'most daring of us' were not content with the old formulations and set about exploring the hold of the ship; (2) 'chance' intervened so that they discovered a way out of the hold and up to the bridge; (3) this process was 'the normal effect of organization' within the hold and had little or no connection with the disputes and amusements taking place there.

We must frankly admit that all three hypotheses strike a sour note in a work such as mine. Stressing discontinuity, they tend to undermine the possible significance of Jesus of Nazareth for us today. The quest for his meaningfulness over the course of twenty centuries, together with all the efforts at proselytism and society-building, clearly belongs to the dicussions in the hold.

As I have already noted, this hasty generalization from Teilhard's image is given the lie elsewhere in his work. This is particularly evident when we examine a basic notion in his view of evolution: the notion of *threshold*. If Jesus of Nazareth somehow constitutes a 'threshold' in the history of humanity and the universe, then he must possess the features typical of any and every 'threshold'. Those features derive from the fact that the world of meaning, like the physical world, is a *quantum* world. In other words, things begin to acquire perceptible energy or meaningfulness when a certain level of quantitative increase is crossed.[27] In the ascending process of evolution, then, we find that a 'threshold' has two complementary aspects: (1) seen from 'below', it is no threshold at all since it seems to be an unperceptible continuation or addition of what went before; (2) seen from 'above', however, this imperceptible increase or addition, unlike similar ones that went before, opens up a world of new and different perspectives. There is an apparent break in continuity, a discontinuity of some sort.[28] The constants studied by sciences dealing with the 'lower' circle continue to be observed, but the 'higher' circle gives rise to new cognitive disciplines designed to master the new perspectives that have been opened up.

In his image of humanity's passage from the hold to the bridge of a ship, Teilhard de Chardin is alluding to a threshold crossed by humanity in our own time. Indeed he may be alluding to the crossing of several thresholds that converge into one.

One such threshold may have been humanity's arrival on the moon. Seen from 'below', it basically marks only a small step forward in our ever-increasing knowledge of ballistics over the past few centuries. Seen from 'above' by the vast majority of human beings, it does not even signify a *new* world as yet; it is merely another marvel of the modern world. But within a short time it may well be that the date of our arrival on the moon marked the start of new space voyages and space settlements for the human race, as foreshadowed by our science fiction.

Another threshold clearly was crossed in 1945, and we can perceive it both from below and from above. I refer to the advent of atomic or nuclear weapons. Seen from below, it was just another extension of humanity's arsenal of explosive weapons. That is how it looked to many people when the first atomic bomb was dropped on Hiroshima. Very quickly, however, the view from above became clear. It was obvious that we had crossed a threshold. Up to then wars had been a painful but rather normal occurrence in the history of our planet. They had never placed the whole planet in jeopardy, and along with plagues and natural cataclysms they had served as a cruel but effective check on the growth of the world's population. Now we suddenly were faced with a new and very different type of 'war', if the same term can be used at all. Far from bringing some sort of special benefit to some group, it would mean the annihilation of our planet itself.

Along with this situation we see the rise, if not of new 'sciences', of new elements in the 'art' of politics. We hear fundamentally different calculations regarding the possibility and potential danger of brushfire wars and other wars both hot and cold. We wonder what level of armaments might undermine the new and delicate balance that has been placed in humanity's hands.[29]

Teilhard's image suggests that humanity has crossed one single threshold, so that now the continuation of life and evolution on this planet is at the mercy of humanity itself. But it is obvious from Teilhard's overall work that the inhabitants of the hold have crossed various other thresholds on their way to the ship's bridge, not only since *homo* arrived on the scene but from the time of the first amoeba and perhaps from the very start (see *The Phenomenon of Man*).

Now let us get back to the discussions in the hold, including those about the significance of Jesus of Nazareth. If we operate with the notion of 'threshold', it becomes obvious that the radical change from hold to bridge cannot be attributed to chance, any 'formal' human organization independent of prior actions and discussions, or the extrinsic appearance of some moral quality such as 'daring' by itself.

What was discussed in the hold, when people still thought they were on dry land? Even disregarding many discussions that seem irrelevant from this distance, we know that all sorts of different discussions went on. I have already mentioned Leibnitz's discussion about the best of all possible worlds, for example. At first glance, particularly in view of the tendency to say that this is indeed the best of all possible worlds, we are inclined to regard such a discussion as a typical example of a discussion in the hold or below decks.[30]

Such is not the case with Paul's concern about an incomplete creation that has been left in humanity's hands, that must acquire its meaning and value from human projects. It seems to be sharpening our sense of smell for what lies beyond, for "the fragrance of the islands *beyond the circle of the horizon,*" for making the best wager with helm and boiler in an uncharted sea.

It all seems to be a kind of 'science fiction' in real life. It is as if travellers, who did not see themselves as such, have been imagining and making up voyages to *utopia*, to 'no place'.

Some readers might fairly ask why I have chosen 'Christian' elements as examples of these alleged 'presentiments'. Wouldn't other elements be just as crucial, if not indeed more crucial, in humanity's ascent to the bridge of the ship? Consider, for example, the efforts of ancient Greek thought to conceive the universe as a whole on the basis of its most elementary and simple factors, which marked the start of science as such.[31]

There are two basic reasons for giving a privileged place to 'Christian' examples in our investigation *here*, quite aside from the obvious one that we are exploring the significance of Jesus of Nazareth. It is all the more important to spell them out here because they may provide new elements for judging how his significance was expressed in the past and how it will be expressed in the future.

Reason 1. Any example from a line of thought alien to 'Christianity' either did not have any decisive influence oñ that portion of the human world that has crossed the threshold of self-conscious evolution or else has somehow been integrated into it, first undergoing adaptation to the 'Christian' world that arose in medieval Europe.

Thus it is not even historically accurate to say that the modern West derives from a mere 'mixture' of Greek currents of thought and Hebrew currents of thought. It is certainly true that it contains elements deriving from both, but the mechanism of integration is not one of mere addition. The Renaissance, for example, entailed a complicated process of integration. It did not merely accentuate the Greek element that had been suppressed or nullified earlier. If we want to understand the Renaissance, the Reformation, the Enlightenment, Marxism, or any other significant element of the modern world, we cannot overlook the period when new peoples entered the territory of Europe and gradually accepted its culture. This process was partially autochthonous and partially composed of a very specific amalgam of elements, deriving from different sources, that made up the 'Christian' cultural structure. The barbarian invaders encountered that structure amid the ruins of the Roman Empire. It accompanied and shaped them over the course of centuries, an extrinsic reality that they gradually introjected.

In a world that was not yet in close intercommunication, the successive thresholds crossed by Western, European culture were closely bound up with a 'Christianity' that was also in the making. That tie has continued to exist even after Europe as a whole ceased to represent a 'Christian' world. Even the most negative reactions to that latter world bear its imprint. Indeed the very negation of the 'Christian' world can be valuable to us for a more authentic interpretation of Jesus of Nazareth and his meaningfulness (GS:44).

Reason 2. This is based on the previous one. Through the communication of 'Christian' elements we can note the strange, dialectical mechanisms that govern historical influences. It explains why I have been putting the term 'Christian' in quote marks.

When we study Christianity back at its sources we notice, quite explicitly in Paul for example, the close relationship between its message and the arrival of humanity at maturity so that it can continue an unfinished creation. Only *faith* makes the human being an 'heir of the world'. Hence only action based on faith ties in with the threshold that Paul sees embodied in the complete following of Jesus. But due to mechanisms we shall have occasion to study in more detail, the 'Christian' world of Medieval Europe was not characterized by 'faith' in Paul's sense. It was more characterized by living 'under the elements of the world', as Paul had put it in his letter to the Galatians. It saw the world as a finished creation, and it made that finished world the norm of individual and societal conduct.

Now let us get back to Teilhard de Chardin's image. If we reject the explanations based on chance and the growing formal organization of human-ity alone, we are left with the factor of 'daring'. We cannot logically consider this daring or courage as some sort of fortuitous energy arising in a vacuum, so we must relate it to the discussions in the ship's hold and admit they were not irrelevant distractions. My hypothesis, then, is that 'the most daring' of us must be those who most felt themselves to be the 'heirs of the world', in line with the basic anthropological *faith* that is part of the Christian message in its pristine sense. And this would be true even though they may have felt obliged, by mistake or necessity, to reject what 'Christianity' seemed to signify or did in fact signify. Thus the Christian message could have been buried like a seed in the soil of the West, retaining its essential nature and then sprouting as an unexpected and distinct plant.

If we set aside the past and look at the Judeo-Christian tradition in its most authentic tenor, we find that it is admirably prepared to 'mount the bridge'. That is not true solely in the realm of thought. In some way that may seem mysterious from 'below'. Western society as a type has come to *think about* evolution just as it begins to possess the *means* and available energy to exert a decisive influence on evolution.

I say that because we find in Teilhard's image two elements, which he did not set up in circuit, that characterize the threshold of the 'bridge': i.e., the *helm* and the *boiler*. We must give a direction to the former and keep feeding the latter. And just as we find a hint of that *direction* in our sources for Jesus' message, so in the societies most influenced by it we find a somewhat unwitting feeding of the *boiler*. As has been pointed out by Harvey Cox,[32] the 'instru-ments' that have appeared in Western civilization have not been accidental. That civilization has displayed its own 'daring'. While it may not always have been well balanced, it bears witness to a society more influenced than others by the critique of religion as ideology that is typical of the gospel message and Paul. Only in this case, as I noted above, the offering of this critique has shifted from the official representatives of 'Christianity' to individuals or movements who felt they were dissociating themselves from Christianity in the very process of making their criticism.

I would remind my readers once again that my aim here is not apologetics. My allusions to Jesus of Nazareth here, when other examples could have been used, are intended to establish a much broader point: i.e., that there is no break in continuity between the discussions in the ship's hold and the view from the bridge, even though Teilhard's image seems to suggest there is. We have mounted the bridge, prepared by past history for the task ahead of us. Seen from 'above', those past preparations may seem rather useless. Looking at them from 'below', however, we can see that they were gradually preparing us, threshold by threshold, for the responsibility of managing both boiler and helm today.

II

Closely related to the foregoing matter is another debatable element in Teilhard's imagery that must be examined more realistically: "The time has come to pilot the ship. It is inevitable that a different humanity must emerge from this vision." He is talking about the vision we get upon crossing the threshold of the deck, about the change *in context* for our thinking today. Humanity must rise to a higher logical level if it is to face its real problems today. As he puts it: "The agitation of the hold is no longer possible."

The crossing of a threshold certainly does open up a new panorama, at least when viewed from 'above'. The most pressing tasks change, along with the associated problematic. But here again Teilhard's image is deceiving insofar as it suggests the easiness of shifting from discussions in the hold to the task of piloting the ship. Such facility does not come readily, nor is it evident on a mass scale. Proof of this is the way that the main political issues today are being discussed by the big powers: the Middle East, disarmament, North-South dialogue, etc. All these issues are being treated as if they were questions 'of the hold'.

Insofar as the vast majority of human beings is concerned, I think it is safe to say that *only one* key point of the transition from the hold to the bridge has been perceived. Even its magnitude and consequences have not been fully appreciated, nor have they managed to promote active, effective militancy. For the first time in human history it is now possible for human beings, a few human beings, to destroy the evolutionary process of the whole planet with the push of a button. Instead of steering the helm of evolution or keeping the boiler fed, humanity seems caught up in the futile agitation of not putting a sudden end to itself with the nuclear weapons at its disposal.

But since the power to unleash those weapons is concentrated in the hands of a few, light-years away from the knowledge and decision-making power of the human masses, the majority of human beings has decided to go on living *as if* the threat of nuclear destruction did not exist. This is particularly true in the badly labelled 'Third World', whose people do not even get to choose the few leaders on whom the potential catastrophe depends. To stick with Teilhard's imagery, it is almost as if the shock of an uncontrollable sea has frightened us back into the hold.

Logically enough, this is even more obvious in thinking of the 'less daring' sort. Some have become immobilized in their thinking, as if that would offer a guarantee of survival. Some have turned to a supposedly immutable nature, for example, hoping to find there some law that will tell us once and for all what ought to be done.

Another example is what we might call *cultural* 'Christianity'. None of our prevailing interpretations of Jesus uses historical and evolutionary reasons to point up the 'suitableness' of his appearance in the time and place he happened to live, with its specific mode of production. Instead of inferring one thing from the other, we prefer to adopt the language of Leibnitz and suggest some sort of 'preestablished harmony' between the mechanisms of evolution and the meaning-dimensions of Jesus of Nazareth both with respect to the past and the future.[33]

Even that isn't necessary, however. For christologies from above,[34] the most frequent ones even today, the Incarnation could have taken place a thousand years earlier or a thousand years later without any great inconvenience. Jesus would still have died to redeem us from our sins, and his sacrifice would have brought us pardon even if brought about by other authorities and different but equivalent historical mistakes. His teaching about the Father and his love would not have varied even if fate had located him in the Egypt of Moses or the Greece of Pericles. His essential meaning and significance would remain ever the same.

It is for this reason that almost all the official declarations of Christianity regarding the morality of different aspects of life seem to display the same difficulty or uncertainty in situating themselves. It is not easy to shift from interpreting Jesus of Nazareth in static, 'fixist' categories to interpreting him in evolutionary categories.

Another weak point in Teilhard's image is the impression it gives that the discovery we make on mounting the bridge will automatically provide us with knowledge of the art of navigation. Once we discover the boiler and the helm, it seems, we will then be able to steer the ship and bring it safely to port. So Teilhard suggests when he alludes to those who have already "smelled the fragrance of the islands beyond the circle of the horizon." But of course that is not the case at all. To most people the relationship *between* boiler and helm remains vague and obscure. Teilhard's image assumes that we have specialists in finding energy and fuel, and specialists in pointing out the right direction; but that is hardly certain. Thus prudence suggests we not try too many learner experiments with the ship, which is carrying us all and hardly sailing on a quiet little lake.

True as it may be that the crossing of the threshold *should* give rise to a new humanity, it is even truer that we human beings today do not possess the *epistemology* we need to face up to the new reality. For centuries we have been engaged in fixist lines of thinking. Such thinking may have been dynamic enough in helping people to pursue human plans and projects; but that does not mean it will now be easy for us to make the effort to *think in a different way*, even though that effort is unavoidable. To put it more concretely, we must now conceive human aims as bound up with a process from which they simultaneously receive both positive and negative impulses, energy, and conditionings.

Modern ecology, then, must become an ecology *of mind*, an epistemology, capable of resolving problems of all sorts. To do this, in terms of Teilhard's image, it must explore how and by what rules the ship moved while its principal 'passengers', its once and future crew, stayed down below in the hold. Here we have the new *context* involved in learning how to pilot the ship. From human history, prehistory, biological evolution, and universal evolution we must learn the basic, perduring mechanisms that have brought the ship this far through numerous shoals and reefs.

Remember my discussion of Paul in Volume III. In a creative effort Paul sought to transmit the human significance of Jesus from the Jewish context of Jesus himself to the context of Greco-Roman culture. But those two contexts were already formed; they were *contexts* in the fullest sense of the word. Those cultures had their ingrained, familiar patterns of thinking and exploring, their own specific categories and epistemologies. This is evident from the fact that Paul does not stop to explain the functioning of the categories he is using. When he employs new, original categories, his readers perceive and understand them on the basis of their own tried and true ones.

That is not the case with us, however. Not even those currents of thought considered more 'dynamic' (e.g., Marxism) operate with evolutionary categories, even though they may accept the evolutionary hypothesis. Indeed the founders of 'evolutionism' presented it as a new 'explanation' of the universe. As such, it is just as subject to Marx's criticism about philosophical views that 'explain' the world instead of 'changing' it as are other views. The fact is that the founders of modern evolutionary theory did not possess the perspectives that are ours today, so they did not fashion a new epistemology that could help us with our present task.

We do not yet possess an evolutionary *context*, but we do sense that the task of fashioning such a context and integrating the significance of Jesus of Nazareth into it is urgent and crucial. In trying to carry out that task in this volume, we must constantly balance two factors: what we need to know about the categories we are employing, and what Jesus of Nazareth could signify in those categories. This new task will seem a little strange, since it does not dovetail with the usual talk about this historical figure. It will also force us to undertake a two-dimensional discussion that may seem a bit dry and at loose ends.

Perhaps Teilhard's image will help us to make our epistemological approach, to explore in a broad, general way the two basic and primary characteristics of an evolutionary line of thought that attempts to grasp the significance of the human being, Jesus of Nazareth, for today.

(1). The first characteristic derives from the very idea of *evolution* in the strict sense. We say that something evolves when we recognize its fundamental unity or oneness. If what appears successively were divided into watertight compartments, as were species in fixist thinking, we would not talk about evolution.

In other words, to speak of evolution is to recognize a basic *analogy*[35] among the mechanisms operative in any of the realms we designate as nature or world. And that is wholly *independent* of the question, insoluble by definition, whether this analogy derives from nature *in itself* (hence economically unified) or from the unity of the knowing mind.

Take for example the supposed analogy existing between anatomy and grammar. It is said that there is a similarity or analogy between the way that bodily organs arise, take shape, and fit together to perform the various functions of life, and the way that the parts of a sentence (subject, verb, predicate, complements) are organized to carry out the different functions of meaning. Moreover, and this is very important, we know that this entails the necessity of informing children learning their language, not only about particular sentences, but also about how to construct correct sentences *in general*. In short, we must teach them grammar, understood here as *metalinguistic* communication, as language about language, as sentences about sentences.

Now there would be no analogy with grammar if we did not assume that in a similar way the different members of the bodily organism arise and develop in terms of some *metacommunication*, not about reality external to the organism but about the organism itself and its anatomy. The science of genetics tells us what the instruments of that communication in the organism are: the genes. From the physiochemical sciences we also know in a general way what these mechanisms of anatomical communication are made up of and how they operate. About the content of the information received (i.e., the *language* of this anatomical communication), as well as how and by 'whom' it is received and then executed, we have no source of information or scientific hypotheses except the presumed similarity or analogy of that language with the communications or metacommunications of human beings and their artifacts.

Of course, the analogy is *only* that: an analogy. In the human being the receptor system is the nervous system. It is the nervous system that deals with grammar, receiving information, processing it, and forming correct sentences. And even leaving aside beings without a nervous system, we know it is not the human being as such who receives and processes genetic information. Moreover, the nervous system through which the child learns how to construct sentences is endowed with 'consciousness', in the strictest sense of the word, of the purpose or final totality to which the construction of sentences leads. That is obviously not the case in genetics.

In *some* primordial *way*, nevertheless, the final totality of the organism must be present in the genetic information so that the latter may deal with the totality of different organic functions and their corresponding organs; so that the reproduction of tissues in the case of a wound or amputation, for example, may stop when the 'totality' of the organism requires it. If that is not what actually happens in reality, we must still *think about* genetics as performing functions with anatomy analogous to those that the human mind performs with grammar. For that is the only way we can continue to *explore scientifically*, to elaborate hypotheses following the same law of economy that in principle guides every scientific investigation.

The following statement by Gregory Bateson comes closest to defining *analogy* as I use the term here: "What is claimed is, first, that in both anatomy and grammar the parts are to be classified according to the relations between them. In both fields, the *relations* are to be thought of as somehow primary, the relata as secondary. Beyond this, it is clamed that the relations are of the sort generated by processes of information exchange."[36] For the moment we shall not consider why relations take primacy over the terms related, simply underlining the principal cause of the analogy: anatomy and grammar coincide in being products of 'processes of information exchange'. Bateson then goes on to say: "In other words, the mysterious and polymorphic relation between *context* and *content* obtains in both anatomy and linguistics; and evolutionists of the nineteenth century, preoccupied with what were called 'homologies', were, in fact, studying precisely the contextual structure of biological development."

The most classic example of such an homology is the comparison of the elephant's trunk with the human nose. It is not simply a matter of the spatial 'relations' between the elephant's trunk on the one hand and its mouth and eyes on the other. The 'relations' in question go much deeper, dealing with the main functions of an organism such as that of respiration. That is why the trunk is 'homologized' to the nose, not to the hand for example, despite the obvious use that the elephant makes of it.

The important point here, noted by Bateson, is that such 'homologies' were not regarded as sufficiently serious, heuristic, and scientific for quite a long time.[37] When Bateson reviews the story of his own thinking in the sphere of different specialized sciences, he tells us that even in the first quarter of this century the application of analogy to relations between concepts, processes, or instruments of different sciences (such as anatomy and linguistics) was regarded pejoratively as a form of 'mystical' thinking by scientific orthodoxy. Bateson adds:

I should not preach this mystical faith in quite those terms today but would say rather that I believe that the types of mental operation which are useful in analyzing one field may be equally useful in another—that the framework (the *eidos*) of science, rather than the framework of Nature, is the same in all fields.[38]

Let us pause for a moment over Bateson's statement. Let us look at some of the basic implications and consequences of this crucial principle, as well as at some of the main forms of resistance to it even today.

First, science does not consist of introducing a *photograph* of the external world into our minds. A process such as that embodied in science is inevitably associated with a search for *meaning*. Rather than being a description, it is an *explanation* permitting some use. We do not talk of science when a person communicates to us the numbers that have shown up on a roulette wheel over a given period of time, for example.[39] The first step in the scientific process occurs when we recognize that something is not *pure* chance, that chance alone, by definition, cannot produce it. What are we to call that something?

I just mentioned the term 'meaning', which is obviously something human. Let us try to be a bit more modest, though we shall see that we cannot escape this sin of 'species pride'. There is a linguistic and rhetorical mechanism that is needed to transmit an intelligible message. It is *redundancy*,[40] the way in which we call attention to the *difference* implied in real information by repeating certain elements of what we are saying. Without redundancy we would emit nothing more than 'noises'. We would not even have language because the sequences would have no meaning. They would follow as do the numbers showing up on a roulette wheel, as do mere accidental sequences.

Science, then, begins by detecting redundancies in nature, by detecting *constancies*—the opposite of chance, which is devoid of meaning by very definition. If there is to be information and a start for science, we must discover some regularity, in a sequence of numbers for example, something that is subject to necessity or a perceptible probability. By the same token, whenever such a constancy is detected, the capital sin of a scientist would be to attribute it to *chance*, to dispense with an explanation on the pretext that it is 'accidental'.[41]

Second, every redundancy or constancy is *codifiable*. Indeed it has to be codified, to be put in abstract formulas, if it is to mark a step forward on the road to knowledge in science. And obviously there will be as many codes as there are observable constancies, unless we can construct 'flexible' codes which, through formal similarities, can 'fit' various sequences, can be tried successfully in them.

Thus the constancy with which an organism is reproduced from one or more living organisms indicates the presence of some 'information' transmitted by the genetic elements. The latter are not some kind of organism in miniature that then grows. They do contain information which, from the very beginning, *deals with the whole organism*. This 'information' will be received, decoded, and converted into different instructions for each and every cell.[42]

The same is true of a map or, if you will, of some operation planned by means of a map. The map is not the territory in miniature. We cannot deduce from the blue color of a map that the actual territory will be blue, or from the paper consistency of the map that we will find paper in the territory to use for a fire.[43]

Bateson rightly points out that such 'coding' and 'decoding' is a 'mental' phenomenon. Here 'mind' is taken in the broader sense to mean any apparatus capable of processing information and acting as a result, i.e., of responding with a difference of a distinct sort to the perceived difference. Thus genetic information operates on the cellular level, sense information operates on the level of organisms endowed with a nervous system, mental information in the strict sense operates on the level of the human brain, and mental information in the broad sense operates in computational systems created by the human brain. There is a formal analogy in all information processes. Even if all that is subjective and information does not operate that way, this is the way we come to know the universe and face its challenges through science.

Third, this brings us to another fundamental step in the scientific approach: the *contextual* element in all information. This does not mean simply that science, in trying to explain the constant behavior patterns of beings, must take into account their contexts and the pressures exerted by them. It also means that 'information' is formally contextual. In other words, 'mind' in the broad sense always offers information about relations existing between a behavior pattern and a context.

Gregory Bateson offers an example connected with the training of a female dolphin (*Steno bredanensis*).[44] When a certain type of conspicuous conduct is desired from the animal, that conduct is 'reinforced' with a reward, with food in this case. Thus the dolphin is taught to *repeat* certain performances, and that is how it is trained. Here we have a context of repetition that is planned outside the animal. The animal submits or adapts to it; but we cannot say for sure whether the dolphin perceives it *as a context*, or simply repeats it mechanically because it brings a reward.

Bateson decided to push the experiment further. He wanted to determine whether the dolphin would be capable of 'recognizing' a context and distinguishing it from other contexts, would be conscious of facing the challenge of establishing a *new* constant relationship between context and the environment. From repetition he moved on to propose another context to the animal: the *creation of something new*. No longer was the repetition of a particular exhibition or performance rewarded. The dolphin was rewarded only when she did a new and different piece of conspicuous behavior. At first the dolphin was quite disoriented by the change because she did not understand the language or logic of reward. Reward now seemed to come by accident. Then, between the fourteenth and fifteenth training sessions, the dolphin seemed to show a great deal of excitement. She had found the solution. When she came out for the fifteenth session, she put on an elaborate performance "that included eight conspicuous pieces of behavior, of which four were new and never before observed in this species of animal." She had come to grasp *the context as such*. As Bateson puts it: "From the animal's point of view, there is a jump, a discontinuity, between the logical types. In all such cases, the step from one logical type to the next higher is a step from information about an event to information about a class of events, or from considering the class to considering the class of classes."[45]

It might be objected that all such examples occur on levels very close to human intelligence, that we would find nothing analogous on more primitive levels, in the behavior of plants for example. But that is not correct. If we think of genetic information, for example, we cannot help but consider it to be 'contextual' information. It is much more primitive, to be sure, since it does not have to do with direct relations between the organism and the *external* context. Even so, the genetic code does not always operate in the identical manner. From the very thresholds of life, it processes information and then acts differently in response to the different challenges posed to the structure of an organism. It has to recognize differences in the organism and then act accordingly. Thus the renovation or reconstruction of tissues, indirectly called for by external factors, will be done differently depending on the mutilation or damage caused by the environment. The information is not a response that is always the same. It is not as if the genetic code periodically, or on the occasion of some variation in the organism, proceeds to display the 'photograph' of the complete organism and then sets about constructing it anew. In other words, it does not act as a billiard ball does when it receives energy from the impact of another billiard ball.[46]

In *performance*, which is characteristic of all living beings at least,[47] we must see a 'mind' in the broad sense: i.e., a system that receives and processes information to serve the totality of the organism. That is why we say that the organism adapts, and adapts as a whole.[48] And that is why Bateson, in the passage cited earlier (p. 31), says that in such processes the *relations* are primary and the things related are secondary.

As we shall see further on, this is also true to a large extent in the molecular combinations of inorganic chemistry. We shall examine the supposed *performance* of Maxwell's demon to produce negative entropy.[49]

Where have we been going with all these reflections? We have been discovering that the basic hypotheses that have led science to knowledge of evolution and its mechanisms are bound up with a process of projection or retrojection by us on every level of the universe. We project or retroject the mechanisms operative in us human beings on to those beings that have preceded us, on to 'the primordial'.

Perhaps the human mind has no other key to apply to the universe except that of its own fundamental laws. Perhaps here lies the origin of the 'analogy' we believe we perceive in things themselves. In any case, it seems that we must agree with Bateson's conclusion: since the mind is the only means of information about that reality we possess, 'analogy' is our heuristic instrument *par excellence*, the one that enables us to know the rest.

Since that seems to be the case of necessity, why do so many scientists who accept evolution reject that *analogy* which we repeatedly come across in their own working hypotheses?[50] Why is it that so far the *fact* of evolution, once accepted, has not generated a new epistemology?

If I am not mistaken, the answers to those questions will bring us to the second characteristic of a line of thought that is capable of grasping evolution and making that comprehension the norm for the new tasks facing humanity.

(2). Jacques Monod claims that "the basic premise of the scientific method" is "that nature is *objective* and not *projective*."[51] Yet a few pages later in the same book, *Chance and Necessity*, he states that one of the fundamental characteristics common to all living beings without exception is "that of being objects *endowed with a purpose or project*, which at the same time they exhibit in their structure and carry out through their performances . . . " [52] Yet this conclusion and his continual use of purposive explanations do not stop him from choosing a strange criterion for judging the scientific value of any hypothesis: i.e., the *anti*-analogical character of the hypothesis.

At the high price of falling into another logical contradiction, Monod makes this assertion: "It necessarily follows that chance *alone* is at the source of every innovation, of all creation in the biosphere . . . It is today the *sole* conceivable hypothesis . . . And nothing warrants the supposition—or the hope—that on this score our position is likely ever to be revised. There is no scientific concept, in any of the sciences, more destructive of anthropocentrism than this one . . . "[53] But what does 'anthropocentrism' mean, if not the very course we have just followed in our reflections? And that course was dictated to us by the development of science itself, as Bateson made clear to us. We find ourselves forced to introduce the 'human' notion of information into the most remote and abstruse mechanisms of the biosphere.

I said that Monod falls into a second logical contradiction here. It cannot make any possible logical sense to maintain that "chance *alone* is at the source of every innovation." No novelty or innovation can come from chance alone, unless we label anything and everything as novelty. The 'innovation' detected by science is an interruption in a constancy, the birth of a new and more complex constancy, the appearance of a redundancy (i.e., precisely that which escapes chance, which does not result from it).

Whence comes the aversion of some important scientists to those premises that seem to be necessary if we are to construct an epistemology capable of both explaining evolution and taking over its reins? Disregarding reasons of a more indirect or instinctive nature,[54] we note that the more noticeable and accelerated progress of science in the last few centuries was characterized by the setting aside of the 'problems' of purpose, values, and humanism, i.e., by the rejection of *anthropocentrism* in the realm of observation and explanation. The sciences grew and developed into more and more disciplines, with more and more specific instruments, by turning their backs on the overall analogy of the universe that derives from, or converges in, the human being. The scientific boom coincided with the developing and perfecting of instruments of observation and measurement; and those instruments became increasingly specialized to deal with the countless inherent differences in the objects whose constancies were being explored. Indirectly at least, the stress that had been placed on the search for 'final causes' did prevent the exploration of those constancies for centuries. Strange as it may seem today, the sciences did at one time suffer at the hands of 'humanisms'.

Yet it is clear that *another* anthropocentrism accompanied and conditioned the progress of science; and it was even worse because it was more partial and unbalanced. As Bateson points out: "Science never *proves* anything."[55] He is using the term 'proof' in the strictest sense here. At bottom the 'verifications' of science are *techniques*. When the discovery of a constancy in our observation of phenomena leads to a perceptible increase of effectiveness in the *means* at our disposal, the hypothesis is assumed to be proven until a different hypothesis comes along and proves to be even more effective.

Here we obviously have an anthropocentrism that is all the more dangerous because it is disguised. With the creation of new instruments, scientific specialization has concealed the fact, perhaps even from science itself, that its procedures were destined to end up with something like an immense robot that would give its possessor powers the latter did not have. Viewing itself as value-free, science has in fact modelled a human being dominated by only one goal: more power. The aim is to possess and enjoy the material resources of the planet at an ever-accelerated pace. Of course there are values spurring scientific investigation and determining what is to be investigated by science of a more objective sort; but those values are in fact the ones most opposed to evolution.

However humane or inhuman we may judge the scientific progress of the last few centuries and our own day, we cannot deny that *certain types* of scientific hypotheses could only be created and elaborated in opposition to anthropocentrism and analogy. That simply *had to be* the case. Remember that the analogies running through evolution find similarities of a 'formal' order among the different planes of reality. Thus the element 'information', which characterizes evolution at every level, establishes only a *formal* similarity when we compare, for example, the directives governing genes with the directives governing the neurons of the human nervous system.[56]

If we assume analogy between the primordial and the further developed, which is perfectly logical in dealing with an evolutionary process, we can overlook the 'material' differences. And here I mean 'material' as opposed to 'formal', the former being the actual content involved. The mechanisms and constancies appearing on the different levels are in fact very different. Indeed they are so different that they must be detected and examined by different processes of sense information, hence by different sets of instruments. For example, you don't arrive at an accelerator of subatomic particles by perfecting a telescope.

That is why I think Teilhard de Chardin is basically correct in formulating the following *general* principle, which embraces the whole range of scientific knowledge about the process of evolution: "*In this world, nothing could ever burst forth as final across the different thresholds successively traversed by evolution (however critical they be) which has not already existed in an obscure and primordial way.*"[57] This complex affirmation of analogy in diversity will be, cannot help but be, basic to everything that follows in this volume. Its consequences, including its christological consequences, will surface in the following chapters. Here I simply want to offer two observations that will help my readers to understand those consequences correctly.

First, I want to stress that we should not expect to find 'the same thing' we find on the human level (for example), or a miniature version of it, when we go further back in the course of evolution. We will find only a similarity, a trace of what characterizes certain human processes. Thus anatomy is akin to a 'primordial' grammar. Social legislation performs a function that is formally 'similar' to the function performed by genetic inheritance on a more primordial level. *Just as* genetic inheritance automatically ensures certain characteristics and behaviors, leaving the rest free for experimentation, *so* social legislation does something similar. Through its sanctions it ensures, as automatically as possible on the properly human level, the homogenization of certain basic behavior patterns for the sake of societal survival, leaving other patterns free for experiential processes of trial and error. The analogy, then, is formal; it would be a crass mistake to use the same set of specialized instruments to look for genetic constancies and legislative constancies.

My second observation is even more to the point here. Note again that the analogy lies in the 'formal' rather than the 'material'. It does not lie in the individual aspect of a being or event. It is not the 'pinpoint' occurrence or reality but the process that produces it and the attendant information about the *relations* that have to be maintained with other beings and functions. It is not a specific pine, horse, or human being that is compared, that can prove to be analogous and hence heuristic. It is the *relations* that are primary, as Bateson has informed us. If we are to find analogy, then, we will find it between the photosynthesis of a pine, the digestion of a ruminant, and the agriculture of human beings. It is there that we may detect the general *redundancy* of nature.

To the extent that we particularize and substantivize—and we must do that in a balanced way—we lose the capacity to find analogies and should give up any such pretensions. This is particularly obvious when we look at the course of *history*. Napoleon, for example, is not 'analogous' to anyone or anything. We can find likenesses and differences between him and any other historical personage. The case is different with the *Napoleonic Code*, the legal structure created in his era and influenced by him. It has a lot to do with earlier processes of formulating rights in the human past, and even with more 'primordial' forms of structuring species and organisms at earlier stages of life and prelife.

This second observation is of crucial importance for our topic here. On the human level there surfaces, or at least shows up more clearly, a factor that seems to challenge the claims of evolutionary thought: i.e., *freedom*. If we focus on very short spans of time or very specific geographical locales—i.e., adopt a 'pinpoint' focus—the factor of freedom will tend to disrupt our knowledge of processes and hence be deceptive. The concentration camps of Hitler's Germany, for example, will cause us to doubt that there ever existed the obvious human process of augmenting legal protection for individuals over the centuries, in the place of merely physical protection. Yet that process and tendency becomes obvious and clearcut if we take a long enough span of time: e.g., from earliest human times to our own day.

One could speculate similarly on the short life of the Greek democracies, which were destroyed by Philip of Macedon. One could conclude that any society granting majority participation in government affairs is bound to become the victim of some society with a more authoritarian form of government in a relatively short time. But longer time-spans oblige us to introduce more variables into this 'pinpoint' fact, and we then see that our earlier inference is not valid.

In short, we must look at long periods of time and broad areas of space to see how the historical intentions of individuals and groups—the fruits of freedom—are conditioned by the great forces underlying the human universe. Only then can those historical processes be integrated into the generalizing framework of analogical thinking.[58]

III

We now see that the challenge posed to our thinking by evolution is more complicated than we had expected. We must move from easy analogy to a demanding process of differentiation. It is important to realize, however, that this process is typical of human thinking. It is, in fact, a form of meta-analogy, of synthesis if you prefer.

Remember Bateson's remark that analogy was regarded as mystical thinking when he began his scientific career. He summarized his later view as follows: "I believe that the types of mental operation which are useful in analyzing one field may be equally useful in another—that the framework (the *eidos*) of science, rather than the framework of Nature, is the same in all fields."[59] He then goes on to stress the importance of using both loose and strict thinking: "As I see it, the advances in scientific thought come from a *combination of loose and strict thinking*, and this combination is the most precious tool of science."[60]

Loose thinking is the kind that takes off on the wings of analogy, thus escaping the narrow methods, calculations, and instruments of a specific science that specializes in observing the constancies of a single field. It is the type of thinking that was downgraded as 'mystical' when Bateson was young, and that is still discredited to a greater or lesser degree today. Strict thinking, on the other hand, turns its back on analogy and tries to grasp the specific constancies of a given field, creating a set of instruments suitable for the field in question and dissociated from any and all formal similarities. Bateson calls for the necessary interaction of both types of thinking if humanity is to engage in the conscious continuation of evolution. Both are required if we are to promote an 'ecology of mind'.

That brings us back to points considered in Volume I (Chapter X, pp. 258 f.). Remember the basic principle of ecology in our current sense of the word, the one by Ralph and Mildred Buchsbaum that is cited by E. F. Schumacher in *Small Is Beautiful*:

that an environmental setting developed over millions of years must be considered to have some merit. Anything so complicated as a planet, inhabited by more than a million and a half species of plants and animals, all of them living together in a more or less balanced equilibrium in which they continuously use and re-use the same molecules of the soil and air, cannot be improved by aimless and uninformed tinkering. All changes in a complex mechanism involve some risk and should be undertaken only after careful study of all the facts available. Changes should be made on a small scale first so as to provide a test before they are widely applied. When information is incomplete, changes should stay close to the natural processes which have in their favor the indisputable evidence of having supported life for a very long time.[61]

It is easy to perceive and accept the logic of that view in theory, but not in practice. Consider, for example, the equilibrium between humanity as consumer and earth as producer insofar as population is concerned. For centuries nature maintained that equilibrium by means of epidemic diseases and high infant mortality, not to mention human wars.

An even more basic and radical contradiction of the principle is present human behavior. Desirous of magnifying the results of their projects at any price, human beings view and handle natural and cultural things in an extremely manipulative way. So even though it does not take much 'imagination' to perceive the principle, the human mind must be 'educated' to this prudent view of land, plants, animals, things, and the global human context.

Schumacher himself points up the need for this change in outlook, the danger of now considering the land and its creatures as *nothing but* 'factors of production'. I would like to quote him again here, italicizing the remarks that are relevant to my discussion in this chapter:

They are, of course, factors of production, that is to say, *means-to-ends*, but this is their secondary, not their primary, nature. Before everything else, they are *ends-in-themselves*; they are meta-economic, and it is therefore *rationally justifiable* to say, as a statement *of fact*, that they are in a certain sense *sacred*.[62]

It should be obvious that there is a close connection between this statement by Schumacher on the need for an ecological mentality and Bateson's view of thinking analogically about evolution. Viewing certain natural elements as sacred seems to be the 'mystical' type of thinking that Bateson was alluding to. What is more, it seems to be necessary if we are to check our tendency to view everything around us as merely *means* to our plans and ends, those ends focusing solely on ever-increasing quantitative use of natural resources. Respect for environmental contexts calls for a more qualitative view of values, an attitude of utmost respect for the complexity of nature as if it were 'an end-in-itself'. Schumacher's adjective 'sacred' does not refer to a religion or a specifically religious attitude. It has to do with the capacity to absolutize, or better, almost absolutize, certain valid and sure things we are tempted to destroy by merely using them as our instruments.

Now what is the best example of something that cannot be regarded as a mere instrument? Is it not the human person, at least insofar as the individuals of the human species are concerned? Monod denigrates 'animism'. But what is 'animism' if not the result of the tendency to 'personify' the universe, just as our tendency to 'depersonalize' the universe destroys it as an environment for the human species?

By a different route we reach the same basic conclusion if we follow Bateson's thinking. The source of analogy or redundancy in nature is bound up closely with the functioning of the human mind, with the interaction of strict and loose thinking. A world populated with analogies is a world of anthropomorphisms and anthropocentrisms. Only in such a world can human beings feel respect for processes, seeing them as similar to those they respect in themselves and in human relations.[63]

Finally, in both cases the scientific and rational is integrated with the world of meaning and values, precluding a separation that would sooner or later be suicidal. Schumacher would have us look at things *as if* they were 'sacred' or 'ends-in-themselves'. Of course they are not human persons; they continue to be in the service of humanity and its projects. But there is a deep-rooted Manichean tendency in human beings, not only to divide human beings into good and bad, but also to divide beings into *things* and *persons*. Insofar as this division takes over the human mind, everything that is done with 'things' is justified by science. The only moral issue then is whether the human intentions and aims in using them are good or not.[64]

The tragedy does not lie in the fact that people claim that the end justifies the means, or more precisely, that the end justifies the means *so long as the latter are truly effective and the former good*. The tragedy lies in the fact that the effectiveness of the sorcerer's apprentice turns against him and destroys him.

How is balance to be restored? Clearly by regaining *respect* for things we have downgraded as mere means. That can be done naturally and spontaneously, which is the only real, effective way, only when we 'personify' them, when we perceive the *analogy* between their processes and our own.[65]

It is not a matter of prescinding from science, of fancying or imagining what does not exist. It is a matter of habituating ourselves to a mental process that is necessary and reasonable (not rationalistic), and that is inextricably bound up with the progress of science itself. Loose thinking, thinking by analogy, is an essential component of that mental process, either because nature itself is 'redundant' in reproducing structures and processes that are formally similar, or because the structure of our mind orientates us that way in the search we all must make to unify and explain the reality we must face.

•

Let me now briefly link these remarks with Jesus of Nazareth and what follows in this book. As I pointed out, the basic epistemological principle that must guide us in our study of the present-day significance of Jesus of Nazareth comes from Teilhard de Chardin, and we have been investigating its ramifications in this chapter. The principle itself is this: *"In this world, nothing could ever burst forth as final across the different thresholds successively traversed by evolution (however critical they be) which has not already existed in an obscure and primordial way."*

This means that we must combine and integrate strictly historical thinking about material differences that separate the primordial from the more evolved with analogical thinking that perceives the formal similarities of an overall process in evolution.

Jesus is part of that process. He is integrated into it and conditioned by it, just as he conditions the process to the extent that he is meaningful. In Volume II we examined the 'material' content of his history with the more precise instruments at our disposal. We studied what happened at the 'pinpoint' moment when Jesus of Nazareth appeared on the scene, preached, acted, died, and then gave his disciples a glimpse of the eschatological through their experiences of his resurrection.

In Volume III our analysis of Paul forced us to abandon the 'pinpoint' uniqueness of Jesus of Nazareth and introduced us to the 'formal' dimension, where the redundancy of the overall process shows up. If Teilhard de Chardin's principle is reasonable or correct, it is there that we shall see the historical Jesus linked up and related with all that has been and will be occurring in the evolutionary process. The same must hold true for any person whose meaningfulness holds interest for us from the past.

Jesus, who appeared at a given moment in the process, should have some similarity with 'primordial' forms that foreshadowed him and paved the way for him. In the following chapters, then, we shall travel both ways on the road that leads from the primordial to Jesus, and from Jesus to the primordial.

If the past is to be meaningful for the tasks of the present and the future, we cannot evade this search. We cannot turn Jesus into a pinpoint lost further and further in the remote past, nor can we turn him into a vague generality escaping the conflicts of time by virtue of his abstractness.

CHAPTER II

Jesus from the Standpoint
of the Primordial

In the previous chapter we spelled out some of the basic features of an evolutionary line of thought. Readers might justifiably assume that we can now move on to interpret the significance of Jesus of Nazareth in those terms, to explore the meaningfulness of that historical personage for humanity.

But that is not possible. Mere common sense will not help us much, if for no other reason than that we are not used to the meanderings and difficulties of evolutionary thinking.

The relative 'newness' of the topic alone means that various ideas in this area present problems. Some are simply scientific mistakes: *homo* has descended from the monkey. Some concepts are inadequately or incompletely defined: evolution takes place by *chance* plus *natural selection*. And some are clearly misunderstandings invalidated by their own lack of internal coherence: evolution purportedly is "*randomness caught on the wing*, preserved, reproduced by the machinery of invariance and thus *converted into order*, rule, necessity" (Monod, p. 98; my italics).

Moreover, even though biological evolution has left unmistakable traces on our planet, which have been discovered and compiled by paleontology, we are still far from a satisfactory knowledge of the mechanisms that have produced the marvelously complex world of life around us.[66] This is true even of the genetic mechanisms, which are perhaps the best known. Thus evolution is more than an hypothesis in one sense but less than an hypothesis in another sense, since it has not yet offered us verifiable explanations.

This means that we must proceed more slowly than we might have hoped to do, certainly much more slowly than when we examined the possible relevance of Jesus in previous volumes. In those instances we were using categories associated with common sense or our familiar culture. That is not the case here.

In each chapter we will have to lay the groundwork before we can trace out, in no more than a sketchy way, the relationship between the mental mechanisms studied in the chapter and the significance of the historical person known as Jesus of Nazareth. Up to now, as I have indicated, his significance has found expression in fixist molds of thought, which picture the human being as existing more or less unchanged from its beginnings.

As we saw earlier and will see again, certain problems about the origin (creation) and end of the universe did surface to puzzle the biblical writers of both the Old and New Testaments. They were forced to try to solve them with the limited tools they had, and in their efforts we often find worthwhile features. I shall try to prove that those features reveal their full relevance only when they are integrated into categories that allow for their fuller development and expansion.

Right now, however, the task is to lay the groundwork. Even though I am no specialist in these matters, I must try to offer my readers what I feel is more trustworthy and worthwhile in the thinking of others about the mechanisms operative in evolution, as well as about the ability of our own mind to ponder them, understand them, and transpose them, by way of analogy, to such processes as those that reach down to, and take off from, Jesus of Nazareth.

I

Before examining what can be known about the primordial, I want to consider what is regarded as such by those who have elaborated some of the more complete and trustworthy theories about the mechanisms of evolution.

Among those who talk about evolution we find a discrepancy that is more significant than it might appear at first glance. Some (e.g., Teilhard de Chardin) refer to *universal evolution*. Others more discreetly restrict the term to *biological* evolution.

For example, one of the scientists in the second group is the Nobel Prize-winning biologist, Jacques Monod. In *Chance and Necessity* Monod describes the difference between his own thought and that of Teilhard de Chardin in these terms:

> His [Teilhard de Chardin's] philosophy, is based entirely upon an initial evolutionist postulate. But, unlike Bergson, he has the evolutive force operating throughout the entire universe, from elementary particles to galaxies: there is no 'inert' matter, and therefore no essential distinction between 'matter' and 'life'. His wish to present this concept as 'scientific' leads Teilhard to base it upon a new definition of energy. This is somehow distributed between two vectors, one of which would be (I presume) 'ordinary' energy, whereas the other would correspond to the upward evolutionary surge.[67]

This negative judgment is uninformed, since Teilhard spelled out very clearly what he meant by the two vectors and one does not have to 'presume' what he means. It also suggests that something important lies behind the choice between *universal* evolution and *biological* evolution. That in fact is the case.

Monod's statement amounts to a confession. He is telling us quite clearly that the evolution whose secrets he is going to explore in his book begins mysteriously at *a given moment* in the process of universal evolution. It begins at the point when *chance has already been placed in the service of finality or purpose*, though Monod uses the Greek equivalent *teleonomy* to avoid the term 'finality' or 'purpose'.[68]

Now it is perfectly licit to make this practical break in the hypothesis, if for no other reason than that life could have been introduced to planet earth from outside rather than being a product of the physiochemical evolution of the planet iself. But there are disadvantages to this partial consideration of evolution. One of the most obvious is that it disregards a basic scientific fact of our day. Only by closing his eyes can a scientist disregard the fact that the 'web' of physiochemical matter shows no clear break in continuity between the most complex molecules of inorganic physics and the most rudimentary molecules entering into the makeup of a living cell. Clear proof of this is the fact that the transition from the former to the latter is the object of ongoing experiments in laboratories.

Clearly there is something fishy about the attempt to limit one's scientific working hypotheses to the domain of *biological* evolution; and it has to do with the role and capability one attributes to chance, which one leaves in absolute charge of all explanations on the inorganic level. Since it is characteristic of *all* living beings to possess some intrinsic purpose or teleonomy, one presumably must go outside the biosphere to find the reign of pure chance. There the necessity and danger of hypotheses cease. For without teleonomy one can say of the inert realm, as if it were the only *scientific* hypothesis, that only chance is at the origin of all novelty, as Monod does.

But even the world of inert matter does not impress us as one of chaos, which by definition would not and could not have any explanation. Chaos would correspond to what we might expect from 'chance alone'. Yet on the macroscopic level at least, physics and chemistry tell us that the behavior patterns of the realm of lifeless matter display much more regular constancies than do the behavior patterns of the biosphere. The biosphere seems to be much more 'chancy' than does the world of lifeless matter, the latter more closely resembling the functioning of a machine than a game of chance.[69]

That is not all. The very notion of *chance* is anthropomorphic, even if only in a negative sense. It derives from the notion of a human being who suspends or loses control of its purposiveness to some extent, at some level, for a certain period of time. To imagine a *total* chance, however, would be to imagine a world not made; and in a world not made there would be no chance either.

The notion of chance surfaces within a universe where finality or purposiveness reigns, signalling the limits of purposiveness *at each logical level*. If a roof tile falls on the head of a passerby, that does not indicate the absence of purpose. The tile has a purpose, its placement has a purpose, and its state of maintenance or disrepair has an explanation. When we say that the tile injured the passerby *by chance*, we mean that none of the agents associated with the purpose of the tile or its fall could have foreseen the exact moment or concrete result of its fall.

Thus the very notion of *chance*, when used properly, necessarily has to do with the behavior of entities already existing and acting *before* chance 'plays' its role. The fact is that 'chance alone' does not exist, by very definition. Chance refers to a 'negative' quality that is attributed to certain agents. It is not a substantive noun or subject to which we can properly attribute active verbs.

What, then, could Monod possibly mean when he tells us that "chance *alone* is at the source of every innovation" (p. 112)? The first 'innovation', and many more besides, would have had to arisen beforehand for chance to 'play' its role among them. To give a concrete example: does he mean to say that the first molecule endowed with purposiveness or teleonomy, the 'innovation' *par excellence*, arose by chance combination of lifeless physiochemical elements, that this was *one* of the infinite possibilities in the shuffle of 'chance alone' that finally surfaced in the universe? But the use of chance to explain something that suspends chance, that 'catches it on the wing and turns it into necessity', is an attack on logic; on any other plane of reality it would be regarded as an anti-scientific explanation.

Let us explore this further by examining what science calls the laws of thermodynamics, which are said to govern the activation of energy throughout the universe, hence both life and *prelife*. We are particularly interested in the second law, which has to do with a kind of qualitative gravity known as *entropy*, the general tendency toward *the degradation of energy*.

Obviously energy 'degenerates' *for the human being*, escaping from our hands and becoming less and less usable for us even though it remains constant in the universe. But it would be useful to attempt a definition of entropy that is less centered around the human being, if that is possible; to formulate, as it were, a law about things *in themselves*. Though it is only an approximation and far from complete, Francisco Hunneus makes such an attempt in the following statements: "The second law of thermodynamics postulates that the natural tendency of a system isolated from its environment is to arrive at a state in which the maximum *disorder* possible for that system prevails. When the system has arrived at that maximum disorder, it is in a state of equilibrium because the constituents of the system are *indistinguishable from one another*."[70]

Again the term 'disorder' seems to be closely bound up with human purposes, as we shall see. But note that here it is practically equivalent to a notion that we would consider more 'objective': i.e., the *non-differentiation* of the components.

Now to talk about non-differentiation is to talk about the impossibility of communication, and hence about the impossibility of any knowledge. For, as Bateson tells us, "a 'bit' of information is definable as a difference that makes a difference."[71] Thus information, cognitive value, and differentiation are synonyms. Hunneus puts it this way: "For an object to be observable, it must be out of equilibrium with the rest of the environment. Equilibrium means equality . . . So the concepts 'out of equilibrium' and 'distinct from the environment' are correlative and say the same thing."

Citing an example used by others,[72] Hunneus adds that differentiation and cognition not only are synonymous but also produce each other *reciprocally*. The reason is that cognition, in the short or long run, is always bound up with purposiveness. Wanting to know means wanting to differentiate. That is why Bateson says that the basic unit of information is a difference *that makes a difference*. It is a difference serving a function or purpose, altering something in accordance with some plan or project, hence representing a *performance* in the realm of physics, biology, or cybernetics.

It is here that a famous example comes into the picture: 'Maxwell's demon'. The famous Scottish physicist, James Clerk Maxwell (1831–1879), tried to imagine how it might be possible, in principle at least, for the second law of thermodynamics to prove 'false'. First, here is Monod's description of the basic and general situation:

> The 'degradation of energy' or the increase of entropy is a statistically predictable consequence of the random movements and collisions of molecules. Take for example two enclosed spaces at different temperatures put into communication with each other. The 'hot' (i.e., fast) molecules and the 'cold' (slow) molecules will, in the course of their movements, pass from one space into the other, thus eventually and inevitably nullifying the temperature difference between the two enclosures. From this example one sees that the increase of entropy in such a system is linked to an increase of *disorder*: the fast and the slow molecules, at first separate, are now intermingled, and the total energy of the system will distribute statistically among them all as a result of their collisions; what is more, the two enclosures, at first discernibly different (in temperature) now become equivalent. Before the mixing, work could be accomplished by the system, since it involved a difference of potential between the enclosures. Once statistical equilibrium is achieved within the system, no further macroscopic phenomenon can occur there.[73]

It is in this situation that Maxwell introduces his 'demon' into the picture:

> We recall how this hypothetical personage, posted at the communicating opening between two enclosed spaces filled with a gas of whatever kind, was supposed, without any consumption of energy, to maneuver an ideal hatch enabling him to prevent certain molecules from passing from one chamber to the other. The gatekeeper could thus 'choose' to allow only fast (high energy) molecules through in one direction, and only slow (low energy) molecules in the other. The result being that, of the two enclosed spaces originally at the same temperature, one grew hotter while the other grew cooler—all without any apparent consumption of energy. However imaginary this experiment, it caused physicists no end of perplexity: for it

did indeed seem that *through the exercise of his cognitive function* the demon was able to violate the second law. And as this cognitive function appeared neither measurable nor even definable from the physical standpoint, Maxwell's 'paradox' seemed to defy all analysis in operational terms.[74]

In fact, this was not a violation of the second law of thermodynamics. What interests me here, however, is how we might characterize this 'demon' that seems to go against entropy. Here is the key to the riddle as explained by Monod:

> The key to the riddle was provided by Léon Brillouin, drawing upon earlier work by Szilard: he demonstrated that the exercise of his cognitive function by the demon had *necessarily* to entail the consumption of a certain amount of energy which, on balance, precisely offset the lessening entropy within the system as a whole. So as to work the hatch 'intelligently', the demon must first have *measured* the speed of each particle of gas. Now any reckoning—that is to say, any acquisition of information—presupposes an interaction, in itself energy-consuming. This famous theorem is one of the sources of modern thinking regarding the equivalence between information and negative entropy [also known as negentropy or neguentropy].[75]

We are at the heart of our problem. Maxwell's demon is of the utmost interest because it manages to increase differentiation and order in the system without any apparent application of energy from outside the system. The question this raises and the answer to it are voiced by Hunneus: "Is the principle of the increase of entropy of spontaneous processes invalidated when intelligence intervenes? Yes, of course." As Monod points out, and as Hunneus would undoubtedly agree, in the end entropy regains its jurisdiction; but that is not the point. The point is that there exists only one reality capable of winning any victory, however incomplete, small, and momentary, against entropy. That reality or force, involved in any and all transmission of information, is cognition, knowledge, mind, intelligence, or whatever name you choose to call it. Concludes Hunneus: "Intelligence—understood here as the capacity to process information—*is capable of going against the second law.*"

Now why do we say, why must we say, that Maxwell's demon has *processed information*, hence that a 'mind' or 'intelligence' had to be present? The logical answer is: because it has removed something from the pure play of chance. As Hunneus puts it: "If it did not possess information, the demon would have let any molecule move in any direction, with the result that *statistically* the system would remain [better: end up] in equilibrium." In other words, it is logically contradictory to assume that mere chance can *constantly* produce the very same type of behavior in molecules or any other physiochemical element.

Now even though it is statistically unlikely, it is not absolutely impossible that more hot or cold molecules might pass from one enclosure to the other in significant numbers within a certain number of seconds. There would not have to be any *communication* for that: i.e., a transmitter and a more or less 'intelligent' receiver capable of processing the information. But it is downright contradictory to maintain that *chance* has produced (e.g.) a genetic communication that has remained practically invariable over millions of years. And what is one to say when that *performance* is repeated in thousands of cases?

In talking about evolution, people are indulging in a logical trick when they try to separate the physiochemical processes of inert matter from the biological processes marked by purposiveness, communication, and *performance*. Such a separation is untenable. They would like us to think that the purposiveness characteristic of life arose from chance *alone*, as one of many possibilities. *From that point on*, supposedly, everything is explained by the interaction between such purposiveness and natural selection (i.e., the challenge of the outside environment). But that hypothesis, built up against all logic, crumbles as soon as we perceive, already at the prelife stage, the necessary action of 'mind' creating negentropy.[76]

II

At the start of *Steps to an Ecology of Mind* Gregory Bateson puts a set of fascinating dialogues with his daughter. They are called 'metalogues' because they are dialogues about dialogues, and because in the course of the dialogue itself one realizes what the dialogue is about. Using simple language and many examples, which conceal an iron logic, the author puts forth arguments dealing with the most general scientific problems, particularly those relating to the epistemology imposed by evolution and its laws.

The title of the first metalogue indicates that its subject is the second law of thermodynamics, and entropy specifically: "Why Do Things Get in a Muddle?"[77] Put more abstractly, the question is: Why is disorder easier and hence more frequent than order in the (human) universe?

The father's general answer to his daughter focuses precisely on this intimate connection between easiness and frequency: "It's just because there are more ways which you call 'untidy' than there are ways which you call 'tidy'." In other words: if we assume that chance shuffles the possibilities, then there are almost an infinite number of possible disorderly deals for one orderly one. The calculus of probabilities is that there will be many more 'messes' than 'tidy' or 'orderly' situations in the universe.

When his daughter thinks that this explanation is meant as a joke, the father assures her that he is not kidding: "No, I'm not fooling. That is the reason, and *all of science is hooked up with that reason*."

Notice that this whole supposed law is based on the ambiguous, 'dangerous', anthropomorphic notion of 'order' or 'tidiness' on the one hand and 'disorder', 'mess', or 'chaos' on the other. But why should any cold, objective science regard one mix (e.g., of the letters *ytuaeb*) as *disorderly* and another mix (of the same letters: *beauty*) as orderly? As the father points out to his daughter: "Let's look at what *you* call tidy . . . because let's say we can find *somebody* who thinks it is more tidy" another way. They are talking about negentropy, you see, and the daughter finally gets the key point: "Daddy, does somebody have to *say* something like that [i.e., 'this is tidy *for me*'] before you can go on to talk about how things are going to get mixed up when you stir them?" The obvious answer is 'yes'.

This is the problem with the second law of thermodynamics: *homo* must say that a certain type of energy is degraded *for human purposes*, since energy remains constant in the universe according to the first law of thermodynamics. From one transformation to the next, all energy gradually turns into calorific energy. Diffusing into space, it eventually becomes unusable *for any human design* even though physicists must say that none of it has been lost.

Thus the second law of thermodynamics, or the law of entropy, explains something that is important and crucial for human beings even though it may be enunciated in "objective" terms. The father puts it as follows: "They say what they *hope* will happen and then I tell them [with the law of entropy] it won't happen because there are so many other things that might happen. And I know that it is more likely that one of the many things will happen and not one of the few" (Segundo italics).

I want to stop here for a moment to make two observations that are relevant and necessary at this point in our discussion.

(1). We have pursued the track of the primordial and the more evolved in both directions. Moving downward and crossing the boundary between the biosphere and the inorganic, we found unmistakable traces of a primordial form of the human. We have been compelled to project such concepts as 'information', 'mind', and 'performance' back into the most basic processes of matter. Moving upward, we have discovered that even the seemingly most objective notions of the primordial make no sense unless they are hooked up with human purposes and proposals. They must somehow be hooked up with the notion of 'order', which is fundamental for *meaningfulness* (i.e., for the human being).

It should be clear, however, that these convergent results are not *scientific* in the strict sense of the word. They are *epistemological*. They are not a discovery about things but a metadiscovery: a discovery about discoveries. They do not provide knowledge about things. They primarily provide knowledge about the science of things, about how to structure science itself, its hypotheses, and its investigative methods.

(2). This observation will be of crucial importance for what follows. In Bateson's metalogue considered above, the real topic is entropy, not evolution as such. Entropy is *one* of the vectors of the evolutionary process, and it is the one on which Bateson focuses. This helps to explain the rather curious conclusion he draws for his daughter: "I know that there are infinitely many muddled ways, *so things will always go toward muddle and mixedness*" (Segundo italics).[78]

That is true, if the field were left entirely to entropy; but the panorama of universal evolution clearly does not suggest that. Impossible or false as it may seem, things have gone toward order. Or at least toward what human beings, in their pride or self-interest, call order. So let us move ahead by focusing on two examples: one a real one noted by Monod, the other a fictitious one noted in Bateson's metalogue.

Undoubtedly the odds against the living molecule are almost infinite in a world of inorganic chemistry. There does not seem to be a tendency in the universe for such dispositions to 'come up' in the supposed lottery of *chance* transformations of energy. If such a tendency were to exist, we certainly could not talk about 'chance', or '*pure* chance', or 'chance *alone*'. If we suppose that the odds in such a lottery were a billion to one against a living molecule ever appearing, then those odds would remain the same for the appearance of a second living molecule.

Obviously that is not the case. The first living molecule is 'replicated' and manages to conserve the result of chance, according to Monod.[79] It is faithfully translated into millions or billions of copies, just as if that first 'living' molecule were Maxwell's demon.[80] It is as if it took advantage of chance to communicate to some part of its own being the know-how to produce a companion, collaborator, and successor. A scientist would have to indulge in very 'loose' thinking indeed to maintain that chance is thus 'caught on the wing' by . . . chance! If the same thing kept happening in any lottery, even the most elementary 'scientific' habit of mind would suggest to us that someone had 'fixed' or 'rigged' the drawing!

Evolution is an undeniable fact, you see, despite what Bateson tells his daughter. Things have not always gone toward 'muddle and mixedness'. Indeed in saying that, Bateson is overlooking a basic element of his own most original thinking. In the very same metalogue, however, Bateson does offer his daughter a key to the whole notion of negentropy and how we might view it:

> F . . . Sometimes in the movies you will see a lot of letters of the alphabet all scattered over the screen, all higgledy-piggledy and some even upside down. And then something shakes the table so that the letters start to move, and then as the shaking goes on, the letters all come together to spell the title of the film.
> D: Yes, I've seen that—they spelled DONALD.
> F: It doesn't matter what they spelled. The point is that . . . the letters came together into an order . . . they made up something which a lot of people would agree is *sense*.

His daughter knows how that is done and tries to interrupt him, but the father proceeds to give the explanation:

F . . . And they make it look like that in the movies by doing the whole thing *backwards*. They put the letters all *in order* to spell DONALD *and then* they start the camera *and then* they start shaking the table.

D . . . And then when they run the film, they run it *backwards* so that it looks as though things had happened forwards . . . [81]

Bateson tries to impress his daughter with the fact that things never happen that way in real life, only in the movies. But is that true? Is it possible that he has in fact offered us an epistemological key with which to approach the whole evolutionary process?

It seems quite obvious that evolution displays a process strictly parallel to that of running a film backwards. *With the cognitive instruments at our disposal*, then, the only logical way for us to find meaning in it is to run the time machine backwards.[82] In other words, what is last in our spontaneous, naïve vision of things is really first and original as logical and heuristic principle. In some invisible, primordial way purposiveness is mixed in with the chance that seems to hold sole mastery over the physical processes of inert matter; it uses chance and gradually takes charge of it, without ever annulling it.[83]

In sheer logic this evident observation should become a crucial, epistemological principle of science itself. It means that every glance backward at the process of evolution must assume an active intelligence and project from the very start in order to explain how the tendency toward entropy has been overcome—only partially and incompletely, true, but nevertheless steadily.

There is no scientific possibility of working with the hypothesis of universal evolution unless we at the same time acknowledge the generalized operation of Maxwell's demon. If we look at evolution and find that the most complex systems occur at the end rather than the beginning of the process, we are in effect saying that there is only one possible explanation. We must read and interpret the whole phenomenon in reverse chronological order, as Bateson and his daughter did in the case of the film.[84]

Thus we find a project present in the universe even before the process made room for the appearance of an intelligence supported by a developed nervous system and capable of consciously shouldering the battle against entropy as its task.

I am not saying thereby that the universe has been created, or that this necessary reversal of time is a philosophico-scientific proof for the existence of God. But I do think I have shown that the very hypothesis of an evolution is bound up with an epistemological premise, explicitated or not, that serves as the necessary ground for all the hypotheses of science. The premise is that entropy and negentropy coexist from the very start of the universe, each on its own plane as we shall see further on. As we go further back into the past, negentropy shows up in ever more primordial and primitive forms; but they are always *mental* forms. This invasion of mind[85] seems obvious when we look at the evolutionary process in reverse, but improbable in the direction of history;

just as the order we found in Bateson's example of a movie film had to be there at the beginning, even though any future calculus based on the most economic hypothesis—chance—predicts the victory of disorder and non-differentiation.

Something else has also been made clear, I think. When teleonomic or purposive terms are used by those who claim to hold strictly to 'the postulate of objectivity', they are not using improper language to make their arid calculus comprehensible. Nor need they be ashamed of language that is 'all too human' or anthropomorphic. What they are doing in fact is following the epistemological thread that originated the discovery, the order of the working hypotheses used by science.

Let me cite a specific example. Let us look at a comparison between the fossils of the primitive horse, *eohippus*, and the skeletal structure of the present-day horse. A notable difference between their extremities is that the *eohippus* fossil shows five toes on each foot whereas the skeleton of the modern horse has a hoof, which can be nothing else but the extremity of a single toe. What happened in the time between the two? What working hypothesis enables the scientist to re-create the (partial) evolution that goes from one extreme to the other, and that would be confirmed or verified by the intermediate fossils at our disposal today? Note the following statement by Monod:

> . . . the initial *choice* of a certain kind of behavior (for example, in the face of attack from a predator) *commits* the species irrevocably in the direction of a continuous perfecting of the structures and *performances* this behavior needs for its support. It is because the ancestors of the horse at an early point *chose* to live upon open plains and to flee at the approach of an enemy (rather than try to put up a fight or hide) that the modern species, following a long evolution made up of many stages of reduction, today walks on the tip of a single toe.[86] (Segundo italics)

Is this a questionable, *ad usum Delphini* explanation of a process that was discovered in the reverse direction, a feeble attempt to avoid anthropomorphism and stick with the 'postulate of objectivity'? If we do not start with humanity and analogies based on the human, then 'objectively' we must start with nothing but molecular biology. According to that, genetic variations can come about only by 'error' or some 'alteration of the instructions received'.[87] And if that were the case, we would have to conclude that the above-mentioned process would have taken place, perhaps did take place, with or without a predator, with or without open plains, and most importantly, without any individual of the species being able to commit the species in a definitive way or to 'choose' running and flight for it. Chemical chance should be the *only* thing responsible for what happened,[88] whether the selective pressure of environment existed or not.[89] The 'absolute freedom' of genetic chance, 'blind liberty' in the face of external challenges, logically rules out any particular explanatory hypothesis.

In other words, the very hypothesis formulated by Monod to explain the prehistory of the horse runs counter to the 'postulate of objectivity' he deems basic to scientific thinking. His hypothesis really begins at the end, asking the only question that can lead to verification of what happened in the remote past: *What purpose* is served by the fact that the leg of a horse ends in the tip of a single toe? And once that is answered: *What purpose* is served by the fact that the horse runs more in open plains? And so we must continue down the lane of purpose or finality.

There is no point in wearying my readers with more arguments about this arid subject.[90] So let us get back to the basic theme of Bateson's metalogue with which we began this section.

Note that its implications, as we have explored them, are valid for the existence of any type of *order* in the universe (including that of science):

(a) Order means an essential relationship to purpose and, in the last analysis, to the human being who determines it.

(b) This order is the basis of any real scientific hypothesis, not only in the realm of living beings but also in the universe as a whole, despite the protests or inconsistencies of a scientist.

(c) If this order exists, then it is by definition the first thing.

To get back to Bateson's example of a lottery drawing, chance alone does not allow us to expect the ongoing appearance of a word like BEAUTY, or a line of poetry, *in a permanent way*. If that meaningful order appears and perdures, then it must have been there at the start of the stochastic process, limiting it as its intrinsic purpose.[91]

And what is to stop us from leaping over the intermediate steps and concluding that the final meaning, the one that gives order to all things from the very beginning (even those left to chance), is not BEAUTY but JESUS? Suppose that 'Maxwell's demon', which produces negentropic effects at the molecular level, is a 'primordial form' of what Jesus of Nazareth signified at the level of energy handled by the human being and brought to its maximum potential of concentration, efficacy, and meaningfulness!

At first glance such a statement may seem to be sheer madness. Considered more closely, it is but the simplest application of the principle of universal analogy, which is basic to science, that we saw in the previous chapter (see p. 63). It is Teilhard de Chardin's principle: *"In this world, nothing could ever burst forth as final across the different thresholds successively traversed by evolution (however critical they be) which has not already existed in an obscure and primordial way."*

Thus it is not foolish or sacrilegious to ask what might have been the evolutionary impact (from the end point) and the primordial forms (from the starting point) of the project launched by Jesus of Nazareth in Palestine about two thousand years ago, the strange reality which the historical Jesus himself described as the *kingdom (or reign) of God*.[92]

In this connection in might well be useful to cite a christological text formulated by Vatican II. It finds its inspiration in Teilhard de Chardin, and it is one of the first attemps to formulate, discreetly but officially, the significance of Jesus of Nazareth in evolutionary terms: "The Word of God, through whom all things were made, himself made flesh and dwelling on earth (Jn 1:3.14), entered the world's history as completely human being *[perfectus homo]*, shouldering and recapitulating it in himself (Eph 1:10). It is he who reveals to us *that God is love* (1 Jn 4:8), at the same time teaching us that the fundamental law of human perfection, and hence of the world's transformation, is the new commandment of love" (GS:38).

By now my readers, already perplexed by the novelty of this volume, may be wondering what one is to make of such a statement vis-à-science. I will try to answer that question in section IV of this chapter, but first we must overcome another problem by going back to the scientific side of the matter.

III

Let us consider briefly the hypothesis that denies intrinsic finality or purpose in the evolution of the universe, that limits itself to biological evolution and tries to explain what happens once 'chance alone' has produced beings endowed with purposiveness or teleonomy. How does it work?

Monod himself suggests to us that the advantage of starting the study of evolution with the biological sphere is that one can avoid purposive hypotheses in trying to explain the origin of life. For a scientist, then, evolution begins when chance puts him face to face with beings endowed with teleonomy.

Not everything is explained in evolution, however, by the fact that all living beings are endowed with this curious quality or capacity. And this for a very simple reason: the purposes of the organism have no communication with the genetic code. To go back to our example of *eohippus*: if it 'chose' to flee its predator rather than facing it, it was not able to communicate that intention to its genetic system; nor could the latter, unaware of the decision, encode in the genes the more appropriate means for flight on the open plains in order to benefit descendants of *eohippus*.

That is why Darwin, unlike Lamarck, postulates the existence of a second factor in his evolutionary hypothesis: 'natural selection'. Thanks to it, some forms of life that do not manage to adapt to their environment disappear, leaving the field open to those genetically 'accidental' forms that are more fit for survival. We thus get a process resulting in *the survival of the fittest*, a phrase coined by Herbert Spencer and endorsed by Darwin.

When Darwin put forth his basic hypothesis, little was known of the genetic mechanisms familiar to science today. From our standpoint today, then, Darwin's more naïve evolutionism may seem closer to Lamarck's view than to that of Darwin's successors today, who are rightly called neo-Darwinists. Monod would be one.

But Darwin himself, Darwinists, and Neo-Darwinists are linked by a common epistemological premise they share: the quest for hypotheses that will, as far as possible, eliminate or reduce anthropomorphic and purposive explanations. As Monod puts it, they adhere to the 'postulate of objectivity'. They cannot deny that all living beings are endowed with teleonomy, but the role of the latter in evolution is reduced to the minimum: the 'will' to survive, the fight against the common enemy, death. It is *blind* nature that selects among the strugglers. Everything not due to the will to live is done by *natural selection*, which likewise arises out of a chance external to the individual, in the form of an environment it must face. Unintentionally it imposes challenges that only permit some to survive. And the survivors, *by that very fact*, are called 'the fittest'.[93]

Over against this epistemology, common to the various forms of Darwinism, Bateson proposes a different one. It is more suitable or 'fitter' for thinking about the problems posed by biological evolution in a scientific way.[94] And, in fact, it is not new or unheard-of.

As Bateson points out, it is paradoxical and historically curious that another scientist and thinker, Alfred Russel Wallace, reached seemingly very similar conclusions just before Charles Darwin formulated his theory of the origin of species.[95] But Wallace's concept of *natural selection*, unlike that of Darwin, was not based on a Lamarckianism retarded by chance. It was based on the principle of a huge natural (homeostatic) *circuit*, akin to that which governs the temperature in the boiler of a locomotive for the sake of the *performance* expected of it. Interestingly enough, Bateson suggests that scientists would have been years ahead in the investigation of evolutionary mechanisms if they had started with Wallace's explanatory hypothesis (i.e., his epistemology) rather than with Darwin's.[96]

Let us briefly consider the main scientific reasons why Wallace's overall explanation commands greater respect than that of Darwin.

The *first reason* has to do with the concept of *survival*. As I noted above, this concept proposed to offer information about the conduct of all living beings, with the barest possible minimum of teleonomy. The problem is that such a minimum may prove to be inadequate, to be no explanation at all.

The concept of survival would function as an explanation insofar as the pressure of environment remained stable at a level where the possession and maintenance of a genetic anomaly, which has resulted from environmental chance and proved to be 'favorable', constituted a 'matter of life or death' for the individuals of a given species over a long period of time. But such an explanation presumably ceases to function as soon as the external pressure eases. This latter point is important, since a mild environmental pressure could not select. The only means of selection available to the environment is mass death. For, as experts in genetics tell us, the 'favorable qualities' acquired by an organism have *no means of communication* with the genetic code.

To go back to Monod's example: it is very possible that individual members of *eohippus*, who had not genetically increased their velocity, could not survive the pressure of environment at a given *moment*. A very demanding environment might have wiped out those who did not have the genes that chanced to be appropriate for speed on the open plains, such as those that produced the anomaly of lost toes on the foot. But the species seems to have gone on specializing in that trait long after it had ceased to be decimated by its predator (in whom we do not see a parallel process with regard to speed). At first glance, it seems as if speed became an 'addiction' of the species. The species continued its specialization even when it was no longer faced with the threat of immediate, total extinction.

According to Wallace's hypothesis, the process would have been more complex. It might have been something like this. When the first members of *eohippus* endowed with a more favorable mode of running managed to flee successfully, the predator changed its prey. If the predator survived as well, then we must suppose that it determined to feed itself on animals who survived by means other than taking flight: e.g., by reproducing in greater quantity. Meanwhile *eohippus*—and future horse—was free of threat to develop other characteristics (such as size) that would introduce it to a new type of functionality within the whole complex of species and their reciprocal relations.

What was it that happened, then? We find the computer of nature forming a homeostatic circuit where there is survival for the predator, its victims, and those who escape from being victims; where different functions are found in 'ecological' balance. This is not a return to Lamarckianism. It simply means that the teleonomy contained in living beings cannot be defined as a mere tendency to survive. The facts tell us that those who survive are not the 'fittest' in terms of the only admissible biological purpose called 'survival'. The survivors are those that genetic chance renders capable of being integrated into a circuit of reciprocal functions.[97]

In this connection it is worth noting the work of such scientists as Motoo Kimura. After lengthy laboratory investigations in the molecular field, he writes about a 'neutral' theory of molecular evolution.[98] Explicitly challenging the Neo-Darwinists, Kimura asserts that "at the molecular level most evolutionary change and most of the variability within a species are caused not by selection but by random drift of mutant genes that are selectively equivalent."[99]

Paradoxically, then, the introduction of more chance and 'neutrality' in place of qualities of natural selection, far from ruling out purposiveness, demands it by virtue of the greater gap or vacuum left in the explanation. We are thus led to reject 'survival' as the only content of the teleonomy characterizing the biosphere. Selective 'equivalence' makes one thing clear: the differing modes of survival mean that environmental pressure cannot have a definite orientation, hence it cannot explain the direction taken by species in their diversification and evolution.[100]

If one does away with a cause or explanation, one should replace it with another. With the hypothesis of the survival of the fittest, I'm afraid we are not much beyond the level of the medical candidate in Molière's comedy. When asked why opium made people sleepy, his brilliant reply was that opium possessed a 'sleep-inducing' virtue or power.

There is a *second reason*, closely bound up with the first, for preferring Wallace's explanation to Darwin's. Let us take a look at the factor to which 'natural selection' is attributed. It is commonly called the 'pressure of the external environment'.

In basic terms this pressuring environment is obviously composed, *by chance*, of the inorganic world. There are rivers, seas, rocks, and temperatures. For animal species, the environment would also include the energy sources they need for life: chemical substances deriving from the organic world itself, particularly from the vegetable world. Existing or non-existing vegetation will thus come to play a crucial role in the 'natural selection' of animal species. The situation becomes still more complicated when some animals serve as food for others.

In the Neo-Darwinian hypothesis, then, genetic chance faces a new problem. Though 'caught on the wing' to some extent by the teleonomy of living beings, it crashes up against a second independent chance that governs the external environment of organisms. A chance genetic mutation must prove its capacity to survive in a glacial period or a tropical climate. It must leave a marine habitat, or plunge into it, because of earthquakes, shifts in the earth's crust, and so forth.

This hypothesis introduces as much economy as possible on the level of purposiveness, as one can see. But is it really successful as an hypothesis? Does it really explain what is observed? Let us see.

There can be no doubt that the context or external environment will always exert a selective pressure on genetic chance, particularly in extreme circumstances; that pressure will be eliminative. But what kind of pressure can be expected from a randomly *changing* context? And what sort of 'selective' *results* can come from this encounter of two fortuitous processes?

If we put our logic and imagination to work in line with that hypothesis, it seems we must assume that *over the long run* chance changes of environment will *equally* pressure *all* the specific forms of survival tried by genetic chance— both favorably and unfavorably, and in successive waves. Pure chance, in other words, is a *conservative* element.[101] And in a context of entropy, as the 'absence' of Maxwell's demon suggested earlier, conservation means not the differentiation but the progressive and fatal non-differentiation of all species. As we saw earlier, "statistically the system would remain in equilibrium."[102]

Some readers might object that I have forgotten that Maxwell's demon, the supposed creator of negentropy, is present in the hypothesis, since it grants the teleonomy already existing in all living beings. In that case, however, you must admit that 'natural selection' is not the initial explanation of the evolution of species; and also that it exercises *an ever-diminishing* influence as the process advances and teleonomy asserts itself as a crucial factor.[103]

Insofar as the evolution (and consequent differentiation) of species is concerned, scientists base their knowledge on solid paleontological arguments. There is general agreement that, from the point where life began to leave perceptible fossil traces on our planet, the animal species have been diversifying in a tree-like manner, with trunk, branches, and shoots of secondary and tertiary orders.

Now if we had to take literally the hypothesis of natural selection according to the mere capacity for survival, then the species would appear as successive waves and disappear in the same manner. They would sink to the lowest level from which they emerged, or back into the trunk that would never take shape as such. The chance conjunction of a genetic mutation and a favorable environment would heighten the survival possibilities of a species, while that conjunction lasted. But to the extent that a favorable environmental pressure had specialized the species along the lines of a determined survival, the subsequent chance change of the external environment would cause it to drop or disappear completely again and make room for another species. Unless . . .

Unless the negentropy of a system endowed, as such, with purposiveness were to 'take advantage of' every pressure to interconnect more species in a dynamically balanced circuit. It would be by that means, not by chance or exactly by 'natural selection' of the external environment, that negentropy appears to be growing uninterruptedly in the biosphere of our planet.

Natural selection would continue to play a role, of course, which would be especially visible and decisive on the primordial level. But the scientific facts seem to make it clear that this outside influence is clearly becoming secondary in relation to the intrinsic 'ordering' tendency in the teleonomy of living beings. Only thus can the 'conservative' tendency of pure chance be overcome.

A *third reason* for preferring the ecological hypothesis of Wallace to that of Darwin is the curious fact that natural selection, almost by definition, cannot provide any explanation at all, since it is external. This is really nothing but another facet of the same thing we saw above: the impossibility of chance being anything but conservative, at least in the long run.

When we look at the data provided by paleontology and see the tree formed by the differentiation and complexification of animal species in the biosphere, a question pops into mind almost immediately: If *chance alone* is the player in genetics, why can't it make a species go backward as well as forward on the road of specialization?

The hypothesis of natural selection (acting solely on genetic chance) assumes that a chance mutation permits a species to survive where other forms of the same species could not. Thus the genetic accident of a reduced number of toes permitted *eohippus* as a species to survive when it confronted a predator on the open plains.

We have already seen that it is hard to explain the 'specialization' of the characteristic by mere survival, when the environmental pressure changes. Now we must ask a further question: Why wouldn't an opposite selective pressure lead the species, by way of genetic chance as usual, to go backward in the same trait that was once life-saving but is now harmful or lethal, due to the change in the external environment? Why not go back from one to two or more toes, and escape from predators swifter than the earlier ones by fleeing from the open plains to the mountains? In other words: Why not return to the point of non-differentiation with another species to be saved from the fatal pressure of the environment?

The fact is, you see, that in the hypothesis in question the differentiation or non-differentiation of species is allegedly due to genetic chance working from inside and the external environment working from outside. But is it possible there is another *internal* factor that is not chance? Paleontology, after all, shows us that species, once differentiated, do not turn back.[104] Environmental pressure will often eliminate them, but it will not make them go backward.

It is precisely this that gives the aspect of a tree to the schema of species evolution. Once differentiated, a species, like a tree branch, does not return to the trunk. It goes to the extreme of its own possibilities and either continues to survive or perishes.

One thing does markedly differentiate species from the branches of a tree: the 'extreme' of its possibilities does not depend on the branch alone. The deciding factor will be whether, in the face of environmental pressure, it can or cannot integrate with other species in an energy balance. This will give it the evolutionary *flexibility* that the tree branch alone does not have. In Wallace's hypothesis, then, the reciprocal relations between species will say whether each one of them can or cannot find its 'place in the sun'. If it does, even if only by reproducing more rapidly to serve as food for other species, it continues existing integrated in the circuit, perhaps even being specialized in different species. If it does not, then it disappears as the dinosaurs did.

All this makes clearer the heuristic inadequacy of the hypothesis that attributes biological evolution to genetic chance converging with the chance of environmental pressure; and that thus makes the latter, through the elimination of the less fit, the decisive factor of an alleged 'selection'.

That brings us to a *fourth reason* for preferring Wallace's hypothesis over Darwin's: the *quality* of survival procured by the evolutionary process in its ultimate stages—speaking chronologically at least.

From the *quantitative* standpoint, whatever be the criterion used to measure that quantity, the differences between the thousands of species existing in the animal world do not permit us to attribute a greater capacity for survival to 'the fittest'. As we have already seen, there are thousands of forms of survival. The short life of some organisms is counterbalanced, in terms of the species, by multiplied reproduction. This can be 'surer' than the long life of individuals of other species. Moreover, by means of a limy secretion very primitive forms of life construct coral reefs; and these reefs, from the standpoint of survival protection, seem to surpass what is offered by an anthill or a human society.[105]

If there is indeed a *process* that affects the survival of species, then it must affect the *quality* of that survival. That is what we see when we follow the meanderings of paleontological discoveries. But once again we find that this quality cannot be measured in the species alone, but rather in its mutual, circuit relations with others.

What the fossil finds show us is a survival that is increasingly 'orderly', i.e., integrated with a greater wealth of elements. In other words, with more elements and better integrated elements, so that the integration increasingly frees or liberates its different possibilities. What we have, then, is the movie filmed backwards that father and daughter were talking about in Bateson's metalogue, as opposed to the law of entropy, which says that "things will always go toward muddle and mixedness." [106]

If, in Wallace's hypothesis, the whole of nature must be considered a homeostatic circuit, then the thrust of the evolutionary process is making the 'parts' composing the circuit more and more like the total circuit, like the mental whole that is nature itself. To defend themselves against the pressure of environment, for example, the species rightly or wrongly called higher—the most recent ones, in any case—are characterized by the fact that they 'create' the environments they need.

In this connection Bateson notes a classification that is scientifically un-avoidable, even though it brings us into dangerous terrain that seems to shift with our reflections and pursue them. I refer to the dangerous terrain of anthropomorphism or anthropocentrism once again.

Organisms are homeostatic circuits. Acting as 'minds', they control outside variations so as to adjust to them. At first, the point of control is situated very close to what we might call the vital (teleonomic) center of the organism itself. For example, 'lower' animals do not control the outside temperature. They try to survive changes in it by 'adjusting' the functions of the organism to them. Hence they are called 'adjusters'.

But as the process advances and negentropy grows, organisms seem as if they try to maintain the dangerous variables, of temperature for example, farther away from their vital center. We thus find homeostatic systems that regulate temperature by keeping it stable throughout the body area. To do this, of course, the organism must establish control mechanisms on the periphery of the body, and lines of communication between that area and the center. In other words, we get more complex functions calling for more complex relations with other existing species, if for no other reason than to 'feed'—in every sense of the word—this network of communications. The organism once seemed more a *part* of the locomotive (to which Wallace compared nature). Now it seems more like the *overall* mechanism of the locomotive. These kinds of organisms are called 'regulators'.

But the process does not end there. It would seem that nature is busy trying to produce 'super-regulators'. Let us simply look at the human being, without even discussing the evolution effected in 'the human'. We find that the human being is capable of controlling the temperature, for example, through mecha-nisms situated much farther away from its vital center, on a periphery *outside* that of its own body. Through heating and thermostats, for example, human beings control temperature on the periphery of the buildings they construct for their habitat.

Now what are those 'super-regulators' but *minds* re-creating nature and giving another push to the process creating negentropy, order, and meaning?

IV

The previous section may seem dry and far removed from the topic that occupies us in this work. My hope is that it has helped to make my earlier hypothesis seem less incredible: i.e., that something situated in history, such as Jesus of Nazareth and his project, 'recapitulates'—in the strongest and fullest sense of the term, 'gives meaning to'—the universe.

After all, consider the whole history of humanity in search of meaning, and within it the kingdom of God preached by Jesus. What relation could all that have with a universe which, in a struggle to the death, selects 'the fittest' to survive?

Teilhard de Chardin does not seem to have noted or appreciated Wallace's hypothesis. But with good reason, and still within the Darwinist panorama, he proposes an important correction of what would appear to be its central postulate. He writes: "The egocentric ideal of a future reserved for those who have managed to attain egotistically the extremity of 'everyone for himself' is false and against nature. No element could move and grow except *with and by all the others with itself* [Segundo italics] . . . The outcome of the world, the gates of the future, the entry into the super-human—these are not thrown open to a few of the privileged nor to one chosen people to the exclusion of all others. They will open to an advance of *all together* . . . "[107]

Let us replace 'all together' with a term more suitable from circuit epistemology—say, 'all integrated'. We then will have a summary of everything we have seen so far about the evolutionary process from the primordial level. We will also have the basis for the assertion that love—more and more emerging and clear in the higher forms of negentropy—constitutes the qualitative vector of survival that is present in universal evolution from beginning to end. And, as Teilhard correctly defines it, this love identical with the more clearcut forms of negentropy is a risky 'synthesis of centers'.[108] It is only to this value that the whole reality we know, from its most primordial to its highest forms, slowly bows.

Now if we want to find out what relationship Jesus and his project of the kingdom might have with the process of universal evolution, we must do several things. *First*, we must reaffirm what our reflection in this chapter has shown us, since it constitutes the epistemology with which we will have to interpret the significance of Jesus of Nazareth. Then we must take two steps: (1) situate the central historical data we possess about Jesus in the context of the global process we are studying; (2) extrapolate that concrete historical happening which we have already situated, as a transcendent datum, in terms of the reality of the universe.

This chapter has brought us to the conclusion that we must break down the barrier which tries to separate biological evolution from universal evolution. If Jesus is an integral part of the evolutionary process, he must be so as a higher form of that other primordial factor embodied in 'Maxwell's demon' and creating negentropy from the beginning of the universe.

Moreover, if the selection exercised by nature is akin to a homeostatic circuit in which all the elements must be integrated in dynamic equilibrium, as Wallace suggested, then evolution cannot help but consist in a progressive enrichment of the system. *More elements* must be integrated into it in the process, and those elements must become more *integrated*. As they are integrated, more freedom must be left to their creative centers, with all their chances to be right or wrong. Thus "mental" nature shifts from being a nature of things to being a nature of natures: i.e., a nature of persons. This is the line of progress in order, meaning, and negentropy.

In this chapter, then, we must take the two needed steps with regard to Jesus of Nazareth. And here is where we do it.

(1). First, we will examine the concrete characteristics of his message and project. My readers obviously possess the material examined in Volume II and elsewhere in order to do that, so I shall merely recall the data we established and developed there.

The first thing we find in Jesus' history is a project: the kingdom of God as a substitute for the order actually existing in Israelite society. The plan of God announced and inaugurated by Jesus basically consisted in the full humanity of those who had been deprived of it, mainly by mechanisms of marginalization and exploitation that were grounded in religious ideologies.

Why was that sociopolitical order of Israel unjust? Why did it have to be replaced in the eyes of God and his prophet, Jesus? We need only look at two things to find an answer: the concrete plans of God announced by Jesus; and the most important part of his proclamation, the parables, which unmask the ideological mechanism of existing oppression. The existing sociopolitical order was unjust because the 'circuit'—which every society is—did not integrate the majority of Israelites, or did so inadequately.

The term 'marginalization' itself indicates a merely peripheral integration. Those groups or persons were part of society, and it was not simply a matter of being more or less removed from its centers of power. Marginalization will depend, of course, on the type of society and how work and the goods deriving from it are distributed. In Israel the shameful, dirty work was left in the hands of specific groups, the very ones who met with the sympathy and benevolence of Jesus: publicans and prostitutes.

Marginalization also meant that a large part of the society was poorly integrated. Every ideological device was used to lay on it all blame, disdain, and rejection, just as power and the justification of it were concentrated at the other extreme. The poor in general, whom Jesus wanted to make happy in the inauguration of the kingdom that would free them from their present situation, were regarded as the 'sinners' in Israel. Which means that society integrated them to the extent that they stuck to the lowest level of participation in the material and spiritual goods of society. This also explains why the labels of 'subversion', 'destabilization', and social or political 'agitation' might be applied to Jesus. He wanted to integrate the poor, with their initiative, freedom, and rightful claims, into society. But they were, negatively speaking, the pillars of society. They gave coherence and sense to the kind of society existing, and their sinfulness was the explanation for it.

Such a society—and what society is not like that somehow?—would have to have a large dose of almost genetic 'flexibility' in order to take a forward step on the road of negentropy: i.e., to integrate all its members in a better, more central way.

Needless to say, the same things said of the kingdom of God in Israel would have to be said of other societies with similar or equivalent structures of marginalization. There would be specific differences, of course, since those structures might take the form of legally recognized slavery or socially stratified classes. And of course the same would have to be said of the exploitative marginalization we find today on the level of interconnected humanity, which is a circuit of circuits or society of societies.

Looking at the other side, we cannot wholly dissociate that type of socio-political commitment from the attitudes that dominate our conduct in circles that are more restricted but no less important. There is no denying that each plane or level has its own exigencies. Nor can we deny *a priori* the possibility that someone who imposes authoritarian structures at home might be capable of leading a people toward a more democratic regime.[109] But such forms of schizophrenia are always dangerous. If a given way of acting has become deeply imbedded in our habitual conduct, it will be difficult for us to be free of it simply because we change our level of activity.

There is an excellent confirmation of this fact in the moral reflections of Jesus concerning *interpersonal* conduct that is 'consistent' with the kingdom of God. Consistent with the kingdom in the sense that the person who is collaborating with the project should learn how to put it into action right now, insofar as that is possible; and in the sense that the structural and humanizing function of the kingdom is to establish the foundations that will make such conduct even more feasible.[110]

To integrate persons as persons into a rich circuit means to undertake the risky adventure of giving up the ultimate defense-mechanisms that prompt us to adapt our conduct to the conduct of everyone else, to respond to the action of others with a reaction. As we have noted, the human being is a 'super-regulator' vis-à-vis things. But those 'things' called 'persons' usually let themselves be regulated only on the *exterior*. If we want to integrate their *interior*, to possess their innermost richness, we will have to treat and nurture them as the *centers* they are. In that respect we must be super-regulators. To some extent we must lose our own center so that the other person's center may come out and be integrated as such by us.

Such an integration will establish a circuit of two or more super-regulators, pushing even further out the periphery where control is maintained. The human being has already constructed a second, technical nature that is characteristic of it. Now it will put the control it exercises further out, on the periphery of an area that brings together two or more persons, thus beginning the construction of a second—or third—social or cultural nature. The 'thermostat' will be placed at the boundary where the *mutual relationship* of the different integrated centers begins to be affected from the outside. That is what *love* accomplishes.

But letting the other person's center come out means, in practice, curbing our own tendency to the least possible effort, which causes us to integrate others only peripherally. We must take the initiative of *gratuitousness* as our approach so that the other person can be integrated in all its richness as a center. We must give up using others as instruments and make openings for a personal response from them.

This is the conduct alluded to in the most reliable and authentic nucleus of the Sermon on the Mount (mount in Matthew, plain in Luke). Giving up our usual, impoverishing mechanism will mean taking the *initiative* of treating the other person as we ourselves would like to be treated (Lk 6:31). Our calculable, self-interested, mechanical reaction, which uses others as instruments, will be replaced with the *gratuitous* and risky venture on the incalculable. If someone forces us to give up our coat, we are to give them our shirt as well (differently expressed in Lk 6:29 and Mt 5:40). Forced to walk one mile by someone, we will choose to walk two (Mt 5:41). Is it not obvious that these guidelines, at the very least, point the way to the creation of the highest negentropy in the most difficult human relationships, the ones most tending toward entropy? Do they not ask us to integrate our enemies into our own circuit in a far richer and more effective way, when they are in fact the most difficult thing for us to integrate? As if that were not clear enough, Jesus tells us that it is in this way that we become imitators, i.e., creator children, of the God who integrates both the good and the wicked into his beneficent projects (Lk 6:35; Mt 5:45.48).

In the next chapter we will see that this is an orientating ideal, both in itself and in the history of Jesus himself. It can never be turned into a mechanical, habitual mold. Nor can it spare us difficult calculations insofar as the limited supply of existing energy must be taken into account.

(2). It is not strange or surprising, then, to assign the historical Jesus a place, certainly an important place, in the evolutionary process of humanity; and in the evolutionary process of the universe too, since there are no watertight compartments in that process.

Moreover, this does not depend on the religious sphere. Whatever be the *status* of Jesus in the realm of religion, Vatican II found itself obliged to say of him that "he worked with human hands, thought with a human mind, worked with a human will, and loved with a human heart"(GS:22). It is thus that his name is inscribed in human history and the process bound up with its meaningfulness and its energies.

But what happens when Christianity historically takes a further step and affirms the divinity of Jesus, as in the other text of Vatican II noted earlier?

At first glance it would seem that something verified as a *result* is being turned into the source. The product of history is alleged to be the origin of history. That is what seems to permit the divinization of Jesus, to break down the limitations of his concrete historical situation. The question is: Can both things be done simultaneously without mutually destroying each other?

Before I go over this central point briefly, insofar as this chapter demands it, let me offer an historical observation. As readers of Volume IV will recall from my discussion of the divinity of Jesus, there was a lack of evolutionary perspectives and categories when Christianity had formulated the issue. The primary effect of his divinization, then, was the de-historicization of Jesus. Jesus is the origin (Creator) and end (Recapitulator) of the whole universe, apparently insofar as he is above and beyond all the ephemeral conflicts of history.

But that is too high a price to pay. It is precisely the imbalance that the early councils of the Church strove to avoid with their prudent teachings as to how to formulate the divinity of Jesus. Declaring Jesus to be God, they suggested, should not mean a sort of *immobile*, atemporal absolutizing of his historical figure.[111] But for a long time that is precisely what it did mean for many Christians.

As we have seen in the texts of Vatican II, a more balanced view, one more faithful to the origins, reintroduces Jesus into history, hence into the overall world process. The text of Vatican II which says that love is the law of universal progress or evolution begins with a declaration of Jesus' divinity, but it ends with his fully historical existence: "The Word of God, through whom all things were made, himself made flesh and dwelling on earth, entered the world's history as completely human being,[112] shouldering and recapitulating it in himself. It is he who reveals to us *that God is love*, at the same time teaching us that the fundamental law of human perfection, and hence of the world's transformation, is the new commandment of love" (GS:38).

I would say that this 'christology from above' dovetails completely with a serious 'christology from below'. But for the sake of my readers, I must here apply the linguistic principles set forth earlier in dealing with the divinity of Jesus, when I asked what 'play' of language was involved in stating that this completely human being, Jesus, was also God[113] in the fullest sense of the word.

First, in the statement 'Jesus is God', the information does not move from an already known predicate to the still ambiguous, historical figure of Jesus. It is the concept of divinity, with its special features applicable only to a singular, that must be filled with attributes arising out of the concrete history of Jesus. Which means that any 'cosmic' interpretation of Jesus must begin with what we know of his history, not with what we supposedly know about what God is or may be.

Second, the two statements, 'Jesus is (completely) human being' and 'Jesus is (completely) God', are not on the same logical level. If they were, we would be led to 'mix' in Jesus properly human powers and capacities with others supposedly proper to God. The *higher* level of language is a statement about the *lower*, a metamessage about the historical Jesus. To say that the human being, Jesus, is God, then, is not to turn him into a demigod, an 'apparent' human being, a being 'above' the conflicts and problems of history. By the same token, the *higher* level is not a mere exclamation of admiration or a mere mark of my feelings. Its function in anthropological faith is to *elevate* the concrete values perceived in the history of Jesus to the category of absolute, and to wager that to them the entire reality of the universe bows and submits in a personal way.

It is through these two linguistic elements that Jesus reveals to us that 'God is love'. It means that the whole reality of the universe—through evolution—bows to the absolute value that gradually surfaces in all the manifestations of negentropy, its primordial form. Or, to use Bateson's image, it means that the world we see around us is actually a movie filmed backwards, in which love was there first, and then run backward to be made a task for the human being.

Chapter III

The Primordial from the Standpoint of Jesus

We have seen the discovery, in Jesus, that *God is love* takes on cosmic dimensions. We have learned that the universal principle of all *negentropy* is to be sought in that same first love. But our first reaction to that discovery might well be that everyday reality must be governed by some sort of anti-God. The overwhelming weight of experience, of what goes on inside us and outside us, shows us the universal work of the other principle, the principle of *entropy*. We constantly experience the bitter taste of the degeneration of energy into ever-more undifferentiated and unusable forms.

We are right about that, for the discovery we made in the last chapter cannot claim to deny what is all too evident: i.e., the seeming victory of entropy. In a universe where energy remains constant, we daily experience the crushing weight of the conclusion drawn by Bateson in his metalogue: "So things will always go toward muddle and mixedness."

It is what Teilhard de Chardin calls 'the law of big numbers', the law of quantitative victory, that leaps before our eyes and fills our own direct experience. By comparison, the emergence and rise of negentropy in the universe seems more like abstract speculation and a utopia.

From its very start, the Bible had to confront that mystery: a universe, supposedly resulting from the loving and ordering will of God, but in fact invaded by a strange and corrosive evil. And it had to confront that mystery without the benefit of evolutionary categories, which led to some interesting consequences.

We know that the first writer or school of writers responsible for a major portion of the oldest books in the Pentateuch was the Yahwist. The Yahwist accounts are characterized by the frequency and colorfulness of their *etiological* accounts, among other things. Etiological accounts are those which purport to inform us about the origin of things that are part of our normal, daily life.

Right after the narrative about the creation or ordering of the world, the Yahwist feels obliged to attribute to *the human being* the disconcerting but real state of the world created by God. This is done in an account dealing with the first act of disobedience of humanity.

The fact is that human existence has death as its end, that the earth is niggardly in offering its fruits, that suffering and restrictions accompany the most natural aspects of existence (e.g., sex relations and birth). And if all that is not due to an anti-God, then it must be due to humanity itself. At least no other alternative seemed possible for biblical theology at this first stage in its attempt to explain things.

It is not just a matter of *suffering*, however. As we have seen, entropy is even more closely related to the notion of *sin*. It would really be false and wrong to claim that the sin of Adam, as related in Genesis 3, is identical with what theologians would later call 'original sin'. Such an identification, at least in the full sense of the hereditary transmission of a *fault* rather than merely painful difficulties, certainly does not hold for the Yahwist.

Paul does what the Yahwist does not do in Genesis, and he attributes what he does to Genesis. It is part of his effort, carried out in an *anthropological* key rather than a cosmological one, to show how Jesus restores human existence from within, an existence that had been in bondage to Sin and Death. At least Paul goes far enough down this road so that later Christian theology, basing itself on him, will identify the sin of Adam with a mysterious sin that is not personal but nevertheless real, radical, and 'original' in each and every human being.

Worth noting is the fact that so much power is attributed to this sin, with which the human being is born, that up to a certain point even the redemption effected by Christ cannot overcome it. The reconciliation effected in Jesus can gain 'pardon' for it, but it does not succeed in wiping out its anthropological consequences. Even after the redemption, the human being continues to be subjected to *concupiscence*, i.e., the tendency or inclination to do evil.[114]

That is the second step, but it will not suffice. The New Testament authors themselves, including Paul, will have to go further. Because of the magnitude and radicalness of the 'result', they will somehow feel obliged to exculpate the human being to some extent for this universal disorder. Not because the human being is not a sinner, but because entropy itself seems to render it incapable, on its own, of introducing such an enormous imbalance. Explaining that universal factor by one sin, or by human sins alone, did not seem to dovetail with the smallness of the 'space' in which human freedom operates.

So the New Testament took a third step, which seems to bring us close to Manicheism. It appealed to preternatural principles to explain the presence of that negative tendency. The author of John's Gospel, for example, will write about 'the prince of this world' (Jn 12:31; 14:30; 16:11).[115]

Even earlier is a Letter to the Ephesians, whose Pauline influence is not disputed even though his authorship is. That letter shifts the opposing principle from inside the human being to the dimensions of the universe (or even further): "Our struggle is not against *flesh and blood* [metaphor for the inner limitation of our creaturely being] but against the *principalities*, against the *powers*, against the *rulers* of this *dark world*, against the spirits of evil on high" (Eph 6:12; 'prince of the empire of the air' in Eph 2:2).

Here the cosmic dimensions of the power of evil compel the writers to envision a plurality of anti-God elements holding the universe in their power. Such language is not alien to Paul himself. In one of his own most original contributions, where he writes about universal resurrection, Paul elevates the realization of the kingdom of God to cosmic dimensions: "Then the end, when he [Christ] will hand over to God the Father the kingdom, after having destroyed every *principality*, *domination*, and *power*. For he must reign until he has put all his *enemies* under his feet. The last enemy to be destroyed will be *Death*" (1 Cor 15:24–26).

As we saw in Volume III, Paul likes to personify the conflicting anthropological forces. That is valid enough for the enemy 'Death', but it does not apply properly to the principalities, dominations, and powers. Quite aside from the obvious similarity of the latter terminology to that of Ephesians and the explication of the terms as found there, there is the compelling fact that Paul never mentions those entities as participants in the inner conflict that wracks human existence.

Exegetes generally agree that the early Judeo-Christian Church of Jerusalem soon lost influence to a Christian Church of Judeo-Hellenistic origin. This shift meant it was necessary to translate the significance of Jesus of Nazareth into terms that would be accessible to the prevailing culture of the Greco-Roman world. Very early Paul contributed his own undeniable originality to this process, he himself being a Jew from Asia Minor, an area where the influence of Hellenistic culture was very great. John, too, would contribute relevant features to this tendency much later, probably from Ephesus.[116]

Exegetes also generally agree on another important point. The cultural vehicle that the Judeo-Hellenistic community found readymade for its task was *Gnosticism*. Use of it obviously entailed risks. In fact, the first serious warnings we find in the New Testament against deviations considered incompatible with authentic faith in Jesus (1 Jn 4:1–2; 2 Jn 9–11) seem to allude to inferences drawn imprudently from Gnosticism. Although such inferences do not occur in Paul or John, it is assumed that Paul's allusions to the hostile 'powers' of the air do derive from Gnostic cosmology and eschatology.[117]

One of the major dangers of Gnosticism would become obvious in one of its most typical derivatives, one that would become part of our cultural vocabulary even more so than Gnosticism itself: i.e., *Manicheism*. The latter would talk about a supposed cosmic struggle between God and an anti-God, between good and evil as sheer, unadulterated originals, or, in more human terms, between 'the good' and 'the wicked'. This point is all the more interesting for us here since that would become the paradigm and model for human 'intentionality' carried to the pitch of paroxysm, hence the source of all the justifications for the escalation of linear means that now threaten physical ecology and, even more importantly, our mental ecology.

Manicheism is a frontal assault on any epistemology that seeks to explain and support evolution. Indeed it shows up as soon as we start to conceive entropy and negentropy as *two lines between which we must choose.*

Surprised readers may feel compelled to raise a few questions here. Must we not always combat entropy, simply because it is that? Must we not always seek out negentropy and choose it, precisely because it is that? If it is not a matter of choosing between the two lines, if both have been intimately linked throughout the advances and stages of evolution, does that mean that evil can be 'in circuit' with goodness? Sin 'in circuit' with Grace? Well, surely there is a suggestion that this is indeed the case in Jesus' parable of the wheat and the chaff. The owner of the field not only does not choose, but in fact is unable, to have the chaff uprooted because the wheat would be destroyed as well. He cannot see his initial purpose through unless he shows a certain respect for the *enemy*, for some period of time.

Now let us see what we are told by an epistemology that takes evolution into account, the kind we have been exploring in this volume. What does it have to say about the mutual relationship between entropy and negentropy, chance and order, violence and love?

What if we discover that negentropy *could not* take the quick, linear course of a Lamarckian evolution without destroying itself? And that such is the case because negentropy must integrate *time* into its circuit and, with time, chance and evil?

On the answers to these questions, not on any vaunted atemporal or abstract ideals, will depend all the relations that a wise christology purports to establish between a Christian (anthropological or religious) faith and ideologies.

I

Our projects are generally launched in a straight line from the plane of ideal, or values, or faith, to the plane of reality. We try to leave a copy of the former in the latter. And we want that copy to be unalterable, definitive, and ahistorical insofar as that is possible.

It is not surprising that many founders of cultural, social, or political utopias have more or less unwittingly associated their realization with the end of history. What we do not see frequently is that this has something to do with some of the deficiencies that crop up systematically on their course. But it is really not so surprising that the initial realizations of those projects are marked by the anti-evolutionary factor *par excellence*: inflexibility.

We do in fact tend to picture the binomial, ideal/reality, in terms of cause/effect, in what we have chosen to call the terms of logic. We then complain, of course, that reality does not accord with logic, that it is resistant to logic. But what *logic* are we really talking about?

In *Mind and Nature* Bateson broaches our question in a chapter with an ironic title: "Every Schoolboy Knows . . . " In one section he tells us that "logic is a poor model of cause and effect."[118] He is talking about our usual, linear logic, which we tend to regard as 'logic' plain and simple.

Bateson's section is important because it reduces to logical terms what we have seen to be essential to all 'mental' phenomena. And remember that 'mental' phenomena are closely bound up with negentropy and needed to explain and then manage evolution. That essential thing, treated now by Bateson in logical terms, is *the effectiveness or efficacy of a circuit*. Bateson notes that "the *if . . . then* of logic in the syllogism is very different from the *if . . . then* of cause and effect."[119]

So what happens in the simplest sort of electromagnetic circuit? Bateson spells it out this way:

If contact is made at A, then the magnet is activated.

If the magnet is activated, then contact at A is broken.

If contact at A is broken, then the magnet is inactivated.

If the magnet is inactivated, then contact is made.[120]

And so it goes *successively*. We seem to have an apparent contradiction: "If the contact is made, then the contact is broken. If P, then not P."[121] How do we get out of the contradiction? What enables us to understand the functioning of cause and effect in a circuit? The introduction of the element of *time*. Every real circuit is traversed by energy, and that entails a certain length of time. Thus P and not P, which seem to be contradictory, are in fact *successive or consecutive*.

There is an old joke that goes: "What is the most essential thing if you want to light a lamp?" The unexpected answer is: "that it be turned off!" Now we suddenly find that joke raised to a crucial and important epistemological level. Everything in the universe operates through *successive activations and deactivations of energy* in circuit.

Now if we look closely at this law of 'realistic', effective logic, which mediates between cause and effect, we will find something even more important. What is implied in the introduction of the factor, *time*, into the picture? Something of incalculable importance. With time we introduce into the process *entropy*: i.e., disorder, disintegration, and death.[122]

Remember what we saw about the respective and complementary functions of genetic inheritance on the one hand and 'mental' homeostatic circuits on the other. We saw that the former deactivates energy by automatically reproducing certain necessary characteristics, while the latter activate energy by producing the necessary dose of novelty through trial and error. And we explained the quality needed for surviving and evolving in a way very similar to the old joke just noted. Contrary to the 'linear' logic of the Lamarckian model, a rapid genetic change would load the 'mental' circuits to the maximum, however favorable it might seem at first glance. It would force those circuits to experience everything as new again, and to readjust all the mechanisms dependent on them. And what is so fragile or unsuitable about that situation? The fact that all the 'mental' circuits of the organism are activated, hence it is faced with nothing but paralysis when some new demand is made on it by the environment.

In other words: if we want to use the innovative mechanisms, the first and foremost requirement is that they be turned off. And here again time is the factor that allows for them to be deactivated: i.e., the slowness introduced into the genetic code by chance.

Perhaps an example from the human realm may help us to grasp this logic, already operative and proper in the realm of the primordial. Let us consider the case of a man famous for a great discovery: specifically Einstein, for his special theory of relativity and then his general theory of relativity.

To begin with, note that we are all too accustomed, badly accustomed, to regarding such discoveries as 'accidents' due to the magic of a personality. We are inclined to overlook or disregard the problems of 'circuit' efficiency posed by such discoveries, hence the consequences of the intervention of time and entropy in the process leading to the discovery and away from it toward new goals.

Let's start at the end for the sake of clarity. It seems obvious that the 'mental' ordering of such wide and dissimilar physical phenomena in one theory should be viewed as a victory for what we call negentropy. So what would we do if we were given the task of pursuing that line and achieving new discoveries favorable to the development of humanity?

For the moment I shall leave aside one thorny question: To what are we to attribute this discovery? What is its cause? Is it due mainly to some genetic factor, or to a specific degree of learning achieved by the individual named Einstein? Let us take the theory of relativity as given and ask where we should go *from* there.

Broadly speaking, we can say there are three basic orientations of *gradual* efficacy. The *first* would be to protect, prolong, and develop the individual organism in which we find this dose of negentropy: i.e., Einstein himself. The *second* would be to develop a second 'Einsteinian' generation to carry on in the same creative line. This could be done through an 'Albert Einstein Foundation'. The best brains in physics would be selected to carry on the specific task of carrying his discovery forward. The *third* would be to '*vulgarize*' or 'popularize' Einstein's discovery. What was a stroke of genius in him would soon become part of any manual of physics, within the reach of any high-school or college student. In short, we would return it to entropy, to a stochastic process based on chance involving millions of undifferentiated students.

One might object that the question is an idle one because we already know the course taken by evolution. But since the latter offers no guarantee when it is manipulated by human beings, and since it does not suffice to know that the evolutionary process generally proceeds that way, let us look more closely at the advantages and disadvantages of each proposed solution.

Consider the *first* solution. Why can't we rely on Einstein himself to continue Einstein? One fact may seem pretty elementary, but it bears recalling here. Many years are required for Einstein's 'mental' circuits and their energy to traverse all the circuits that led him to his discovery. During those years his circuits had to be activated and deactivated countless times. In other words, we have introduced time into the circuit. The latter did not produce an instantaneous click, from which we could expect another one to follow soon afterwards. And to talk of time in the biological realm is to talk of 'age'.

Note that there were only two clicks of genius in the life of Einstein, both of which were in the same life (amplification). Quantitatively that is not much for the brain of a genius. On the other hand, others less gifted than Einstein have multiplied the applications of his theory in a fairly short time. The story is told about a foundation set up to give prizes to the best works in Einsteinian physics. It once sent the winner of the first prize to see Einstein. Einstein sent the winner back, saying he had not been able to understand him. True or not, the story illustrates what I am trying to bring out here.

A discovery, you see, is something like a genetic variant or mutation. The first person to undergo it will have all his or her 'mental' circuits overloaded. The laws of circuit logic will oblige that person to deactivate those circuits wittingly or unwittingly by simplifying. So at some point that person will be incapable of making a long-term critique of all the complex modifications the mutation is destined to have. And *age* will multiply such deactivations.[123]

What about the *second* solution? It is a 'simulation' of a Lamarckian type of genetic inheritance. It would selectively transmit Einstein's discovery for further investigations, and it would transmit it to a 'negentropic' elite of exceptionally gifted physicists. But that solution has just as many drawbacks as the first solution, if not more.[124]

This solution obviously takes care of many of the problems involved with the individual 'time' of Einstein himself. But here we fall back into entropy by the opposite route. The 'mental circuits' of our gifted minority will not be activated enough to keep learning *along the line of Einstein* in a quasi-genetic way.

There will be no continuation of the evolutionary process that produced an Einstein. He put earlier physics on the scale of judgment. That is what made him Einstein. If he had been 'prepared' or 'trained' to carry on Newton, he would never have established his own theory, however 'ready' the 'environment' may have been for it.

So that brings us to our *third* solution. Like the activated magnet in Bateson's example (P), a genius must be deactivated: P = not P. That is not contradictory but *successive*, since we have introduced time and hence entropy into the equation.

Einstein's discovery must cease to be a discovery and become common knowledge: i.e., cheap, deactivated energy. Only then will it gain sufficient amplitude for chance to use it again, to explore a countless 'population' of students and find the one student capable of using it to arrive at a new discovery by way of extension or criticism.

In short, Einstein and his discovery have to be 'randomized', turned once more into an object of chance in order to be effectively continued. Note that I say Einstein, *not just his discovery*. This is the law of a circuit inhabited by many individuals, "all of them living in a more or less balanced equilibrium in which they continuously use and re-use the same molecules of the soil and air . . . "[125]

Here we come to the crucial point. For the process to keep going on, it is necessary that those molecules be always, i.e., consecutively, at the disposal of all. And only the end of entropy, death, can ensure that. The circuit autonomy that has been allowed to enter time and hence has aged greatly must leave its richness to others. Others, with the same molecules that made up Einstein's brain, must be able to begin their journey toward cognition with their own mental processes. Bateson writes:

> With regard to death, the possiblity for death follows first from criterion 1, that the entity be made of multiple parts. In death, these parts are disassembled or randomized. But it arises also from criterion 4. Death is the breaking up of the circuits and, with that, the destruction of autonomy.[126]

This is necessary for renewed progress in the realm of life and humanity. Starting from there, "the system will learn and remember, it will build up negentropy, and it will do so by the playing of stochastic games called *empiricism* or *trial and error*. It will store up energy . . . Finally, the system will be capable of uniting with other similar systems to make still larger wholes."[127]

Thus the only realistic logic of cause and effect must integrate into the same circuit, not only time, but also negentropy and entropy, order and chance, life and death, novelty and accumulation, love and violence, grace and sin.

But note that to integrate into a circuit does not mean to *intermingle*.[128]

II

Mentally we must maintain the clear distinction between the qualitative dimension and the quantitative dimension, while at the same time knowing how to give each its proper place or moment in a circuit integrated by both. That is the only way to *consciously* follow the line fixed by the *unconscious* evolutionary process that leads to us. And this holds true at every level of magnitude, from the individual to society, and from individual societies to humanity as a whole.

We are talking about a *difficult dialectic*, one that is much more difficult and complicated than the kind that surfaces in certain versions of the Hegelian system or the Marxist system. There the opposites involved, which engage in conflict, synthesis, or mutual change of functions, both belong to one and the same plane or dimension. That seems to be our situation when we attend to the vicissitudes of the opposition between master and slave, or between ascending and descending social classes, or between bourgeoisie and proletariat.

Here we have something different. It is a strange dialectic between values and anti-values. To be more precise, in terms of entropy and negentropy, it is a dialectic between principles prevailing on two different levels. Both are respectable in their own way, but not in terms of one and the same criterion of value; for if they are placed on the same plane, they seem to oppose each other as good and evil.

Here it might be instructive to examine the warnings that Freud offers in one of his books. He writes about what might well be regarded as the supreme negentropic message: Jesus' Sermon on the Mount. And he warns about the dangerous results that would ensue in social psychology if this message were simply applied.

First, a few preliminary points deserve mention. While Freud accepted Darwin's evolutionary explanation, there was not yet a corresponding evolutionary epistemology. The mechanisms involved in the biological evolution of species were not yet categories that Freud could incorporate as such into his thinking, though he may have had some presentiment of them as we shall see. Moreover, we are not dealing here with the heart or center of Freud's thought, whether it be considered a therapeutic practice or a 'metapsychology' developed for and out of that practice. In his later writings Freud often abandons his core work to explore, more or less successfully, other areas of life, extrapolating his theories to such areas as art, religion, and social structures.

In *Civilization and Its Discontents*, Freud tried to explain human dissatisfaction with the restrictions imposed by society. It is a rich and yet confused book, which did not wholly satisfy its author by his own admission.[129] Let us see how it might fit in with our theme here.

Freud writes: "Eros and Ananke [Love and Necessity] have become the parents of human civilization too. The first result of civilization was that even a fairly large number of people were now able to live together in a community."[130] These two 'parents' are very different things, though they are equally important and crucial. In Freud's thought here, Eros [love] is the fountainhead of energy, mechanism, or instinct; whereas Ananke denotes a finite energy context with its two connotations of *necessity* and *scarcity*.[131] Let us look at these two 'parents'.

The first is the 'father', Eros. Irrelevant here is the pansexualism that dominated one stage of Freud's thought,[132] for two reasons. The first reason is my own. A broad, unlimited generalization derived from many diverse phenomena tends to destroy itself as a heuristic hypothesis; instead of serving as a possible explanation, it becomes a mere catchword or label.[133] The second reason is Freud's. He tells us that the Eros responsible for culture and civilization, for any community of work or interests, is not the sexual love relationship that finds its maximum culmination in a pair of lovers.[134] Contrary to the love of such a couple, or even family love if we push the matter a bit too far, the Eros responsible for civilization seeks "to bring people together into larger unities."[135] Mere sexual love is not operative at all, or operative only in a restricted or sublimated form.[136]

Now let us consider the 'mother' of civilized societies: Ananke. Freud notes that the Eros behind civilization can operate only by "obeying the laws of economic necessity" that govern psychical energy.[137] In other words, societal culture is based on an 'economic' distribution of the available energy provided by love.

Thus, to move from a small human unity in circuit to a larger one entails *costs*. Freud does not theorize much about the nature of this cost, aside from the sexual restrictions it entails; but he does offer useful examples to make clear the mechanism operative at a more social level. And one of his examples is the gospel precept of loving one's neighbor as oneself, including one's enemies.[138] Freud finds it easy, of course, to point out the extraordinary energy cost of such a rule, especially when applied to one's enemy:

> But if he is a stranger to me and if he cannot attract me by any worth of his own or any significance that he may already have acquired for my emotional life, it will be hard for me to love him. Indeed, I should be wrong to do so, for my love is valued by all my own people as a sign of my preferring them, and it is an injustice to them if I put a stranger on a par with them. But if I am to love him (with this universal love) merely because he, too, is an inhabitant of this earth, like an insect, an earth-worm, or a grass-snake, then I fear that only a small modicum of my love will fall to his share—not by any possibility as much as, by the judgment of my reason, I am entitled to retain for myself. What is the point of a precept enunciated with so much solemnity if its fulfillment cannot be recommended as reasonable?[139]

Moreover, suppose my enemy holds values for society that I regard as anti-values, as positively harmful or bad things: "So long as these undeniable differences have not been removed, obedience to high ethical demands [i.e., the gospel precept] entails damage to the aims of civilization, for it puts a positive premium on being bad."[140]

So the question we face here[141] is: How are we to integrate into a social circuit, in an energy-balanced way, individual circuits that contain differing or even opposed individual or collective values?

Contrary to what Freud thought, the concrete history of Jesus shows us that loving one's neighbor and enemies is not an atemporal, ahistorical 'high ethical demand'. It is not, in other words, a rule independent of an 'economy' of energy (see section IV of this chapter).

Eros is precisely the source of that energy that leads human beings to create ever larger social unities. But that love can have evolutionary value only insofar as it respects the *flexibility* of the evolving organism, be it an individual or a society.

That entails two complementary limitations. First, something akin to a 'genetic code', in this case a 'legal' code, will have to preserve society from differentiations that cannot be reconciled with its cohesion, defence, and preservation. In no society can all the human beings who compose it be integrated into the overall circuit and still keep *all* the possibilities and risks of their own proper circuits. There will always be a difference between the person and the citizen in any society. Second, there can be no discovery, progress, or evolution unless the 'legal' code (whatever its derivation), which supposedly is equally applicable to every citizen, leaves room for what each personal circuit, and only it, can achieve and contribute by being exposed to trial and error. Thus every social achievement will oscillate between the limits fixed for Eros by Ananke, by the necessity and scarcity of love.

But there is more to be noted here. The assumption that a society begins with a legal code, which finds its inspiration in an objective ethic and is valid for all the citizens, is belied by the historical facts. No society originated in an impartial ethic or in a free, egalitarian 'social contract'. Societies have always arisen on the basis of hegemonic structures of love, which were accepted by others as the lesser evil because of scarcity. Thus we have the parameters for what Freud calls 'differences' in the behavior of human beings. These differences are classified by ethics as 'good' or 'bad', without any regard for the conditions that have given rise to them or affected them.[142]

Thus every society permits some individuals or groups to be integrated into it with all or most of their circuits of freedom and love, while allowing the rest of its human members to be integrated only as simplified circuits reduced to the maximum of non-differentiation.[143] From there it is hoped that future developments will lead in a more egalitarian direction:

> The further course of cultural development seems to tend towards making the law no longer an expression of the will of a small community—a caste or a stratum of the population or a racial group—which, in its turn, behaves like a violent individual towards other, and perhaps more numerous, collections of people. The final outcome should be a rule of law to which all—except those who are not capable of entering a community—have contributed by a sacrifice of their instincts, and which leaves no one—again with the same exception—at the mercy of brute force.[144]

It is on the journey toward that ideal, and in the very instinctual structure that keeps uniting and reuniting human groups in ever larger units, that there emerges for Freud, and for us, the basic option faced by Eros. In the narrow space between the two reefs just noted, Eros can venture to try ever richer syntheses and keep moving toward life (negentropy), or return to the maternal womb by renouncing differentiation and risk (entropy) and destroying itself on the altar of a security that is egotistical and fatal. This holds true for individual human beings, individual societies, and societies of societies. So on the one hand we have Eros in its unceasing work of social construction, Eros in its true and specific essence, Eros in the strict sense: the *life instinct*. And on the other hand we have Eros refusing to live, terrified at the cost of scarcity and the exigencies of the reality principle: the *death instinct*.[145]

There has been much debate about what Freud meant exactly by the death instinct, which surfaced in the final stage of his thinking as he himself notes in *Civilization and Its Discontents*. Here I shall stick with what I regard to be the most plausible hypothesis: that this death instinct is to be identified, *first and foremost*, with *self*-destruction,[146] from fear of the difficulties that reality puts in the way of Eros as it journeys toward life, i.e., toward societies with ever more richly integrated circuits.

I realize that, in saying this, I am pushing Freud a step farther than his explicit thought warrants. With his use of the word 'death', Freud himself seems to want to retrieve the place lost by the aggressive instincts to the benefit of Eros. Thus 'death' would be the instinct toward destruction, directed outward *as well as* inward: toward the destruction of others and of self.[147] The specific direction chosen would be secondary.

In his initial reference to the death instinct, however, Freud alludes to *inorganic* indifferentiation or 'disintegration'. This strongly suggests[148] that the destruction of others is a secondary (but relevant and important) effect of the basic fear of opening one's own circuit to them: i.e., the basic fear of loving. Thus the complex known as *sadomasochism* can be explained as a coherent whole. It is the tendency of a human being or a society to impoverish its vital circuit by eliminating variables in others or itself. It is a fear-based rejection of all that one's own freedom and the freedom of others represent for one's own tranquillity.[149] This rejection, like entropy, impoverishes the circuit through non-differentiation, instrumentalization, and reification.

Thus it is in the very line and course of Eros that life and death engage in dialectical conflict. For if fear of risk is a regression to the maternal womb that may be fatal, it would be no less fatal to put 'a positive premium on being bad'. Circuit logic obliges us to introduce both elements or 'instincts' (Freud) consecutively. Death has its 'moment' in the circuit. And acceptance of it, at the right moment, is a source of life just as chance 'caught on the wing' is.

My readers can find the same thing, this time in *iconic* language, in two passages written by a poetic writer who devoted many eloquent pages to entropy in an implicit way. I refer to Charles Péguy.

Joan of Arc, peasant girl and soldier, presents the *negative* side of the entropy factor:

No matter how much we do or say, they will be faster than we . . . It takes only a spark to burn down a farm, which takes, took, years to build . . . It takes years and years to raise a human being, food and more food to feed it, work and more work and the toils and toils of all classes. One blow is enough to kill a human being. One swipe of a saber and that's it. To make a Christian, the plow must do its work for twenty years. To unmake a Christian, the saber need only do its work for a minute. And it's always that way. It's the nature of a plow to work for twenty years. It's the nature of a saber to work for a minute, and accomplish more, and be the stronger . . . So we will always be the least strong, the least quick. We will always do less. We are in the party of those that build. They are in the party of those that destroy . . . We will always be defeated.[150]

But no simplistic conclusion is drawn from these premises. It does not mean that one must stay on the lookout twenty-four hours a day to make sure that entropy is not allowed in. There is a surrender to entropy, a place given to chance, that is *positive*, salutary, and necessary:

There are humans who don't sleep, and I don't like those who don't sleep, says God . . . They don't sleep! What lack of confidence in me! . . . I'm not talking, says God, of those who don't work and don't sleep. They certainly are sinners, and that is the way it should be for them. They are big sinners! They must get to work! I'm talking about those who *do* work and *don't* sleep . . . The innocent babe goes to sleep in the arms of its mother, but those innocents won't go to sleep in the arms of providence. They have the guts to work, but they don't have the guts to sleep. To let the tension go. To relax. To sleep. The poor, graceless slobs don't know what is good. They govern their affairs very well during the day, but they don't want to entrust the governing to me during the night . . . [151]

Night: image of chance, entropy, death. Night: the most difficult thing to integrate into our proposals, goals, and ideals.

III

It is terribly common, in all areas of human endeavor, to refuse what the efficacy of any circuit requires, to refuse to go through night, chance, and death. And it is this refusal that makes unrealistic the human quest for negentropy as such in a straight line, the option for negentropy *against* entropy. This is the source of ineffective, 'ideological' *idealisms*. And it largely justifies Freud's aforementioned criticism of the Christian ideal of society.

In Volume I (Chapter V, section I), I looked at the 'social doctrine' of the Church and its failure to come to grips with the relationship between faith and ideologies. Here I would like to offer another similar example of the same problem: the issue of *human rights*, which is now so much debated on the international scene and so relevant in many societies. Then, in the next section of this chapter, I shall look at the official Church position on the issue, suggesting that it derives from a christology in which the efficacy of Christ is conceived in linear rather than circuit terms. I shall suggest that the Church, once again, is trying to move straight from ideal to reality, to avoid the limitations and meanderings of ideologies which are such a necessary part of the process.

(1). Nothing in *factual reality*—past, present, or future—tells us what the social relations between human beings exactly will be, or what place, function, and scope will be given to each individual in a given society and the whole complex of societies. We are obviously dealing here with *ideals*, with an 'ought to be' that has yet to be planted in reality. Some might prefer to view it as a specific humanist ideal based on certain values that establish what any individual should be granted or refused in any and every kind of society.

No one rejects those 'rights' as 'ideals'. The problem arises when it comes to implementing those values in reality as *legal rights*: i.e., with juridical instruments needing the support of coercive instruments on the one hand and presupposing a certain societal structure on the other. The latter may be only a structure of 'energy' distribution, so that we may know whether it is possible to distribute 'equally' what the ideal tells us properly belongs to each and every person: e.g., their rights as citizens.

In my terminology, I would say we are dealing here with an anthropological 'faith', based on 'witnessing' societies that enable people to keep an eye on this collective pathway to happiness and place a wager on it as being more important than other possible social values. But 'human rights' also constitute an 'ideology', since they also allude to the means provided by law to make them a reality: i.e., courts, a penal code, and coercive sanctions in force at the societal level.

We come to realize that human rights constitute a *faith* today insofar as we see other things of value being subordinated to them in concrete policies. In short, we discover the 'faith' through the price in values that is paid for that ideal. Is a country ready to go to war for those rights, or give up some of its consumption, or set aside a considerable share of its own security and predominance?

But the *ideal* finds expression in a *list* of *rights*. That was true in the case of the American Revolution and the French Revolution. And it was also true after World War II. And a list of rights suggests the legal and peaceful possession of the benefits contained in them.

Here I shall focus on the U.N. Declaration of Human Rights promulgated in 1948. In fairly iconic form that declaration lists the rights or benefits that the society of the future, which it is hoped will be created, will offer each and every one of its members. Those rights include benefits necessary for survival (and actively pursued since the beginnings of humanity) as well as others whose value came to be recognized only in the recent past. Among the latter would be the right to life, the right to an education, the right to freedom of opinion and worship, the right to work, and the right to sexual equality, racial equality, and national equality.

When we take a closer look at the development of those human 'values' into rights in terms of evolution, we find a noticeable similarity to the Christian ideal of love just examined in the previous section of this chapter. We could almost say they are a lay or secular expression of the same ideal.[152] Do they not imply that the ideal society should integrate into its circuit *all* the circuits represented by individuals, in *all their richness and risk* as circuits? Thus the female would cease to be integrated in the usual way: as a circuit limited to 'the labors of her sex', as merely housewife or homemaker or housekeeper. Her creative liberty would be respected in every domain, and she would be integrated into the circuit of global society.

(2). Moving from 'faith' to 'ideology' as a system of efficacy, the issue of human rights necessarily comes down to the means *par excellence* in this area: *law*.

But that is not really how the issue is tackled on the international scene in most cases, although that is where the issue comes up most pointedly. The usual procedure is to start with a declaration of principles accepted by all. Criticism then centers around the relative *sincerity* or *insincerity* of one's adhesion to these principles.

Two approaches are used to make this judgment. One is more direct, one more indirect; both, however, are examples of 'linear' logic. The first approach focuses on violations committed by the opposite camp as so many proofs that it had no real intention of putting into practice the principles it accepted and formally endorsed. The second approach focuses on the price a given camp is willing to pay for the realization of those values in terms of international alliances and conflicts. Supposing that each government embodies respect for those rights or violations of them, one then considers which governments a given country chooses as allies and how far the commitment goes.

Using the first approach, international forums pass judgment on the violations of the Soviet Union as exemplified in its treatment of political dissidents. Using the second approach, judgment is passed on the tendency of the United States to overlook the violations committed by its allied governments in the Third World.

It can be said, without any fear of error, that such criticism is marked by naïveté, if not downright cynicism, on both sides. But here I would first like to call attention to two curious but closely related features of the kind of thinking represented by that regarding 'human rights'.

The first feature is the strange coincidence between the above type of criticism and the obvious tendency within Christianity to maintain a faith as pure as possible, as untainted with ideologies as possible.[153] Here again the parties start from values that are supposedly accepted by all, overlooking 'ideological' differences that might complicate or embitter the debate. Thus no judgment is passed on the humanism inherent in a given social system. It is *assumed*, for example, that both capitalism and socialism aspire to the same values equally, but that some governments in both camps are more sincere and trustworthy in this area.

The second feature follows from the first. To avoid carrying critical judgment and conflict into the realm of each side's ideology, the finger is pointed at violations that can be shown to be such at a glance. In other words, international tribunals composed of people of 'good will' should be able to pass judgment on them simply by consulting a list. What is the result? Debate goes on about the treatment of political dissidents, a respectable minority of persons, while two-thirds of humanity is starving from hunger.

Indeed where or how are we to locate *those responsible* for this situation without entering into the area of ideologies? A whole nation can go hungry, or fail to provide education for its citizens, without any authority at home or abroad having made a decision or actually violated a single right. No one can denounce the mechanism operative here because it does not issue from the theme of 'human rights' as such. So at every international conference we see the most zealous defenders of human rights refusing to structure a global market that will even out or even improve the possibilities open to the poorest countries, which have been exploited up to now.

No one seems to take note of the fact that the right of dissent is not worth much when a person has nothing to eat, that freedom of the press means little when fifty percent of a country's population, the neediest, are illiterate. And there are no tribunals for those rights, either national or international. So in the last analysis human rights cannot constitute a *list*; they entail a work of construction in successive circuits.[154]

We should not be surprised to find, then, that a humanist or religious faith seeking to be judged and validated apart from any and all ideologies turns out to be 'ideology' in the worst sense of the word: i.e., a system of ideas designed to conceal and justify a reality that people prefer not to change, and that is in direct opposition to the values one claims to uphold.

(3). In historical materialism there is the systematic suspicion that the prevailing ideas of a culture are the ideas of the ruling classes. But even that suspicion does not prevent one from falling into the snares of ideology, if one does not detect the mechanism of self-deceit that gradually detours thinking from its straight path. And as we have already seen, the detour or deviation is not exactly due to what Marxism thinks. It does not so much come from the necessary distance between thinking and the concrete as from a 'linear' logic that does not include time and entropy in the circuit.

Let us see how this logic operates in the transition from human ideals to human 'rights' as reality. We all would agree that they are really rights in the proper sense. But we are wrong in thinking that we need only transcribe a *copy* of the ideal in reality. We see ideal as *cause* and right as *effect*, and so we are back in the trammels of a linear logic that poorly reflects the cause-effect relationship.

If we start by looking at the development of a legal right in human history, we find that no one looks to such a right to gain a particular benefit unless there is a penal sanction associated with the law that established it. To invoke an *unsanctioned* right would be, in Freud's words, to put 'a positive premium on being bad'. Yet that is exactly what we are doing when we try to pass off what is merely an ideal as a legal right, when that 'ideal' is not backed up by competent tribunals, well-defined laws, a police force, etc.

Why is that a *trap?* Because what some people possess already is declared to be a right of all, open to them all by way of law, and only by way of law, even though it was not so obtained by the first people to gain possession of the benefit in question. The latter got it *by other means*. Now those who do not yet enjoy that benefit are urged and compelled to seek it by way of a specific road that they *know to be closed*, that has already been staked out by the first occupant.

If perchance we are not yet convinced of the excellence of human rights, their proponents offer us the following argument to prove their worth. Notice, they say, that the greatest prosperity ever achieved by humanity has been achieved in that country where human rights are most respected. But that tie-in would also have to be shown in the past. And the greatest champions of human rights *today* did not become affluent by wielding those rights in the past. The United States did not occupy its southern and western territories by inviting or urging everyone to practice legality. Its movie westerns make that clear to us, if we did not already know it. Just look at how those who are wealthy today solve their conflicts with their enemies, especially those they regard as inferior: e.g., Mexicans, Indians, and Blacks. Then decide for yourself whether the vaunted tie-in or compatibility between prosperity and legal right is true or not.

And it is not simply the matter of using arms or more primitive forms of violence. In every economic crisis affluent countries will employ a policy of protectionism. Then, appealing to the 'laws' of international exchange, which are fixed by the stronger countries, they will effectively discredit what they call the 'unfair' competition of impoverished countries who are trying to protect their commercial market by the same means.

But there are even clearer examples of the supremely 'anti-ecological' mechanism at work on the mental level, and they explain how and why people can pass from cynicism to naïveté. This is one of the most salient features of *ideology* in the bad sense: it becomes naïveté in the oppressor and it is thus introjected into the oppressed.

Here is an example from right here and now. It is easy to show that the mere fact of monopolizing an undue proportion of the planet's basic energy supply, with or without legal rights, constitutes the biggest or worst ecological threat of all. For, unlike the stockpile of nuclear weapons, this process is not stored away and deactivated; it is in full swing, doing its destructive work. If a country with six percent of the world's population is consuming more than forty percent of the goods being produced on our planet, that may well be the clearest and most important example of a *poor circuit*, and a catastrophic factor of inflexibility for the whole human species.

Assuming we are willing to open our eyes to the situation, let us see what happens to certain 'human rights' when we take into account this global circuit that is catastrophically poor in the circulation of energy. It is obvious that the lack of correlative consumption in the peripheral circuits of this system will necessitate a redoubled violent use of external means to maintain an order that is not accepted or tolerated democratically. The defence of human rights that the affluent countries can afford to pay *for themselves* necessarily *entails the systematic violation* of those same rights among the people who must suffer through the economic crises brought on by the system.[155] And it does not matter what strange sort of 'legality' or appeal to the 'preservation of democracy' is invoked to justify it all.

IV

Faced with the above panorama, which merely serves to exemplify the kind of epistemology now operative, one cannot help but be alarmed to hear Christians calling Jesus 'the great defender of human rights'[156] and thinking they are doing him a favor.

One might think at first that this is just a modish propaganda ploy.[157] But my readers would be right in suspecting that it goes deeper than that. In fact, it is a way of systematically stripping Jesus of everything which, from the standpoint of an ideal, could be regarded as weakness, limitation, or concession. It is the continuing application to him, in the name of his divinity, of false kinds of transcendence that end up turning him into a dehumanizing factor.

In short, the more purified of 'ideologies' Christians try to keep their faith in him, the more 'ideological' in the worst sense becomes his significance for today's human being. Here in the case of Jesus, as in so many other areas of human existence, a proclaimed ideal is confused and equated with the means actually used to realize it. The result of that confusion can only be a 'copy' of the longed-for ideal that is systematically doomed to failure.

The attempt, you see, is to deny entropy in Jesus and attribute to him the 'maximum negentropy'. That would be characteristic of him insofar as he is divine. But the denial of entropy in Jesus runs directly counter to everything we know about him, both historically *and* theologically. And we do well to make that crystal-clear right now.

Let us begin by recalling the fundamental identification of primordial entropy with *Sin* in Paul's sense. When we introduce the factor 'time' into the journey of our project toward reality, we note how the accomplishment of that project somehow escapes our grasp more and more. Our accommodation to that non-freedom, rather than any clear-eyed voluntary consent to something prohibited by the law, is what Paul called Sin, symptom or sting of *Death*. And this was a faithful interpretation of Jesus' message by Paul.

Recall also that Paul closely linked this entropic Sin with the *Flesh*, i.e., the human condition. And he tells us that to remedy this situation in each and every one of us, and to liberate us from the law of Sin and Death, "God sent his own Son *in the likeness of a flesh of sin*" (Rom 8:3; see Gal 4:4).

It is important to note here once again that the most tenacious tendency in christology has been the anti-historical one of turning that 'likeness' into a mere negation, which is an impossible interpretation. Thus the Pauline text has been associated and compared with a passage in the Letter to the Hebrews where we are told that Jesus "was tested in everything like us, except in sin" (Heb 4:15).

But the two passages are not identical. The phrase 'like us' in the latter could be translated 'as we have'. But the noun 'likeness' in Romans unmistakably refers to the external 'aspect' of Jesus, to what can be seen in him. And that *visibility* assimilates him, not only to the human pure and simple (the Flesh) of all of us, but also to the human condition *insofar as it is sinful*. That is why Paul adds 'flesh *of sin*'.

Thus there is a relationship between Jesus' life and project on the one hand, and Sin as the deactivation of certain circuits on the other. This becomes even clearer when we look at the supreme deactivation: Death. It is the very one which, on the physical plane, has as its aim the handing over of material for new syntheses to the chance of the future.

Can we say that Jesus, being free of sin, was not 'destined' for death as every human being is? Can we say that if he had been immortal, as was fitting, he would have improved our lot because he would have carried his project, the kingdom of God, through to completion?

Well, in Paul's reflection on the meaning of the death and resurrection of Christ we find two great themes considered together as united: Sin and Death. But christologies separate those two themes[158] because they assume that the divinity of Jesus demands such a separation, even though Paul himself tells us that we are dealing here with a causal relationship. If any interpretation of Jesus is going to take seriously his cross and its relationship to the kingdom, however, it must explore just as seriously the whole issue of Sin as the cause or sting of Death. It must avoid taking any easy way out in handling the issue.[159]

(1). Let's begin with the term 'death'. Once again we note that Jesus' journey to death seems accidental if it is viewed as the result of a divine plan which called for his death, no matter how or why or at what price, so that his sacrifice might redeem us from our sins. Moreover, the most reliable historical data in the Synoptic Gospels caution us against any such superficial interpretation of the reasons for his death, pointing to causes that are bound up with the actual way he lived his life.

To Jesus himself death appears as a sudden, insurmountable obstacle, blocking his own will and his project. If a person is to be somewhat resigned to his or her death, the latter must have certain features. It should not result from some sort of exterior disorder but should sprout—as a bitter fruit, to be sure—from the negentropy flowing from one's life. It is the simple desire expressed by Rilke in one of his poems: "Lord, give everyone his or her own proper death, death flowing from a life in which there was love, caring, and a meaning."

Certainly the life of Jesus was of that sort. But what about his death? He experienced it as an upsetting contradiction to his whole life, as we learn from his last cry on the cross. His cry of abandonment (Mk 15:34) is one of the most historically trustworthy sayings of Jesus in the Synoptic tradition.[160]

Now if Jesus experienced his death as a fall from order into incomprehensible disorder, from a rich project into the entropy of corruption, we cannot evade the issue raised by Paul. He suggests that Death is an intrinsic power operative already in life, that Death introduces an alienation that gradually takes control over everything human. He tells us that Sin is 'the sting' of Death (1 Cor 15:56), and the term obviously alludes to a cause-effect relationship.

This has to be the 'likeness' that Paul sees between the fully human condition of Jesus ('flesh of sin') and that of every *mortal* human being; and it is reflected in the 'law' governing all human performance and achievement that Paul analyzes thoroughly in the latter half of Romans 7.

To recover the total humanity of Jesus, we simply must ask ourselves to what extent he, too, is included in Paul's analysis of the divided human being. That divided being does not understand what he does. As he tries to carry out his project on the way to death, its accomplishment escapes him when he gets enmeshed in the whole zone of performance mechanisms dominated by 'the law of the members'.[161] There, subjected to the mechanisms of Sin, the human being yearns for a liberation from that deadly condition, that 'body of death' (Rom 7:24–25), which takes possession of his or her labors even before it disintegrates the whole biological circuit of the individual.

Is it really possible, then, that Jesus himself and, even more importantly, the kingdom of God are subject to the law of Death? If the answer is 'yes', then it is obvious from the way Jesus had to face his own death and the failure of the kingdom that he did not know it, did not reckon with that fact, and found it totally disconcerting.

There would be nothing strange or surprising about that. The human being's awareness of its freedom seems to promise something very different. If Jesus was completely human, the death of his project and himself, amid the incomprehension of his beneficiaries and the solid resistance of his adversaries, could not help but be disconcerting. It seems to be just as absurd as is, at first glance, the necessity of introducing time, entropy, and chance into a circuit where the human being just barely manages to establish order, purpose, and negentropy.

In Volume II we considered the concrete experiences the disciples had of the resurrection of Jesus, his victory, and the triumph of his project over death. We saw that those experiences were associated in their minds with the 'power' of the kingdom (see Rom 1:4; also Mk 9:1, particularly if we see a postpaschal element in this prediction). Once again I would remind my readers how significant it is that these curious accounts, contrary to all expectations, stress *the difficulty in recognizing Jesus*.

The Gospels give no indication that this difficulty has anything to do with the sensation of coming face to face with something 'supernatural' or 'celestial'. Mary thinks she is talking to a gardener. The disciples on the way to Emmaus think they are talking to a fellow traveller. The apostles out fishing think they are talking to some fellow on the shore. It is certainly Jesus, but he is *different*.

The accounts clearly find it difficult to spell out 'digitally' the precise nature of this difference. So let us try to see if we might not have some more 'iconic' expressions of it. There is a magnificent chapter on the whole issue of resurrection in Paul's first letter to the Corinthians. Paul is answering a specific question at one point, concerning the sort of body a resurrected person might have. His answer goes far beyond the question, however, because he brings out the shadow side of resurrection: the necessity of dying:

Senseless person! What you sow does not come back to life unless it dies. And what you sow *is not the body that is going to sprout* but a simple grain of wheat, for example, or some other seed. And then God gives it a body, such as he will; to each seed its own proper body. (1 Cor 15:36-38; see Jn 12:24)

Isn't that *the difference* that made it hard for the disciples to recognize the risen Jesus and his project of the kingdom, now liberated from Death? If so, then Jesus, like any human being, learned[162] to overcome the scandal of death, to see its meaning and immerse his aims in it. Thus the grain of humanization that is the kingdom had to go through death to liberate stochastically all its possibilities—and so did Jesus with it.

We have already seen a major example of this in Volume III. Jesus and the kingdom of God died like a grain, as it were, resurfacing in something that seemed so radically different as the message of Paul (who was not even one of the Twelve). There are new modes of expression, new concepts, new implications. Not a single significant quote or anecdote of Jesus himself. We are tempted to ask history one of those questions that cannot really be answered. If Jesus had been around twenty years later, would he have recognized Paul as his disciple, and the Letter to the Romans as a faithful expression of his own message?[163] Whatever the answer may be, the point is that any deep, underlying continuity must be paid for. And the price is death, as we have already had occasion to verify. True, deep continuity is to be found in creative novelty, without which the kingdom of God would have remained merely a grain or seed (see Volume III, *The Humanist Christology of Paul*).

But if we accept the fact that death is not an extrinsic, 'providential' factor, then we cannot help but ask several other questions. What 'law of the members' could and should have led Jesus' project to death and almost unrecognizable resurrection? If certain parts of any organism, after some time of maximum activation, should be deactivated and handed over to chance so that the process can continue further, what were those "parts" in the project of Jesus?

(2). These questions bring us back to the whole issue of the relationship between Jesus and entropy, between the kingdom of God and Sin.

Broadly speaking, we can say that the 'enslavement to corruption' noted by Paul enters the circuit of an organism or project precisely through the cracks or openings left by poorly integrated subcircuits, by those subcircuits that have been integrated at a very low price in terms of the overall energy calculus.

Reading the history of Jesus' project in this light, we find two or three elements that clearly point up limitedness or poverty in the synthesis known as the 'kingdom of God'. We find an oversimplification of the contribution expected or demanded of each and every individual, the instrumentalization of persons, the reduction of many to certain group traits. In a word, we find the strain of violence that is part and parcel of all love exercised in a limited world.[164]

In Volume II *(The Historical Jesus of the Synoptics)* we saw that the efficacy and relevance of Jesus' project in Israel was due to the fact that it activated an expectation. From the outside that expectation could well be regarded as simplistic and limited, since it was rooted in Jewish nationalism and its longing for the reign of God over Israel. However rich his project may have been, indeed precisely because it was rich, he could not have aroused sufficient interest in it unless he also resorted to a factor that would arouse enthusiasm and a following proportionate to people's incomprehension, at least partial, of his project's strict demands. This is certainly obvious in the case of his disciples (see Mk 10:35–39).

If the crowds gathered around him and listened to him, if his disciples persevered with him until the end was near, it was partially due to the misunderstandings evoked by the kingdom as an Israelite hope, for which the Zealots also were fighting. That hope appealed to a certain kind of cheap energy or mass energy. Nationalism, greed, adventurism, and simplified recipes were thus a part of the synthesis, which to some extent had to appeal to such things and the cheap energy associated with them.

We are so dominated by a false conception of the divinity of Jesus[165] and its attendant idealism that we would never think of attributing to him any responsibility for that tenacious misunderstanding and its inevitable consequences. It must have been a mysterious, divine strategy, we think. God writes straight with crooked lines. In any case, Pentecost happened at just the right time to remedy all the negative aspects.

But does this view dovetail with the reality of the gospel account? We are told that Jesus was sent *"only* for the lost sheep *of the house of Israel"* (Mt 15:24). For that very reason he restricts the complementary mission of his disciples to them (Mt 10:5–6.23) and expressly excludes pagans or Gentiles.

Was this a strategy or his own deep-rooted nationalism? Everyone will rush to choose the first alternative. But when the Syrophoenician woman requests a miracle for her daughter, Jesus replies: "It is not right to take *the children's* bread and throw it to *the dogs"* (Mk 7:27; Mt 15:26). This response is all the more noteworthy insofar as such spontaneity—Jesus is not speaking lines as an actor on stage—is one of the safest indications of the impact of cultural stereotypes on individuals. And to talk about cultural or nationalistic stereotypes is to talk about *prejudice*: i.e., the poor integration of what is is alien or foreign, as if it were *inferior*, so that it will be better integrated insofar as that supposed inferiority is recognized or admitted. The Syrophoenician woman wins Jesus' sympathy, but not the correction of the prejudice. That is why she says: "Yes, Lord, but *even* the dogs under the table eat the children's crumbs" (Mk 7:28).

Christolgies have accustomed us to equating or confusing in Jesus the 'completely or perfectly human being' of conciliar definitions with 'complete or perfect human being'. So we think he should represent God on earth and the corresponding universality of values. Even reading the Gospels, we can no longer perceive how profoundly and exclusively Jewish Jesus was. Turning him into a citizen of the world, we make him a stage figure. If he insults the Syrophoenician woman, he does so to teach a lesson to future generations: to test her faith and then grant her what she asked.

The *universalism* of Jesus is undoubtedly a happy outcome of his death. As we saw, however, it was not comprehended even during his paschal experiences, although the later concern to place all humans equally before the same 'good news' would be linked up with those experiences (see Mk 16:15; Mt 28:19; and compare with Acts 10:1–11.18).

A second element in Jesus' historical project where we see entropy playing its role is his way of dealing with his enemies, the scribes and Pharisees.

The customary and certainly mistaken assumption is that the *enemies* of Jesus are purely and exclusively such as the result of their bad will, of something that has nothing to do with Jesus at all. And this assumption is held even though Jesus expressly states that his *mission* prompts him to provoke the most profound and cruel enmities (Mt. 10:34–36; also 10:21).

People find scandalous the assertion that Jesus himself fomented 'the class struggle', as we have noted before.[166] The note of scandal is not due to the use of the technical term 'class' for the kind of stratification in the society of Jesus' day. It is due to the fact that people want to place Jesus and God above and beyond the conflicts that divide human beings and cause them to have 'enemies'.

But if we examine the most original preaching of Jesus, we cannot help but find a conflict, not only assumed but sharpened and fomented by him. His statement that the kingdom of God is coming to make the poor happy is not as innocent as it may seem. As we saw in Volume II, Luke found himself with a problem insofar as he employed the term 'you' and had the beatitudes addressed to Christians; so he had to restore the note of conflict by having a set of woes addressed to the rich.[167]

In the circuit that Jesus was seeking to establish in Israelite society, then, the rich could not be integrated in the same way as the poor—certainly not with the same richness and intensity.

But there is much more to it. Why say all that, if not to prepare people's minds for the change? We have noted that ideological elements prevented the conflict of interests from being seen as such by the victims themselves. The whole system of parables, used by Jesus to discredit the authorities who imposed the *status quo*, could not help but bring out the conflict and indicate which side God's judgment leaned toward and why.

As if this were not enough, there is much more to be noted in Jesus' relationship with his 'enemies'. It is sometimes said, hesitantly but correctly, that 'loving one's enemies' implies that one obviously has them. But no one claims that this precept or outlook should lead people to find ways to maintain or accentuate the situation. Yet that is precisely what Jesus does.

This is evident in one of Jesus' most trustworthy and astonishing statements as reported by Mark (4:12). Indeed Matthew felt compelled to rework it so as to at least tone down its scandalous nature. The purpose of the parables in the case of Jesus' enemies is *"so that*[168] no matter how much they look they may not see, no matter how much they listen they may not understand, lest they be converted and pardoned" (Mk 4:12).

Jesus obviously sets conversion and pardon in the context of God's *historical* plan to change who his people are, so that the kingdom can produce its expected fruits (Mt 21:43). He also frames them in terms of God's *moral* judgment of each individual. Yet Matthew finds this citation from Isaiah so shocking that he changes the words that Jesus found in his source (see Is 6:9–10): " . . . *because* this people's heart has grown dull . . . " (Mt 13:14–15).

In examining the historical project of Jesus, we saw that he integrated his enemies into the circuit in such a way that they and their hostile energy furthered the establishment of the kingdom, despite themselves. Jesus *uses* them in this way, doing violence to their persons and reducing their function to one of passionate, inhuman opposition. He opposes them as being hypocrites. But that is exactly the opposite of the ideal he proclaims with regard to dealing with one's enemies (see Chapter 2, section IV, pp. 61–66).

How could Jesus' own systematic practice diverge so radically from the ideal he proclaimed? Is the problem, perhaps, that we expect his practice to be a faithful reproduction of the ideal he is proclaiming? *Once again* we seem to face the contradiction: P = not P.

But now we know what factor we have to introduce into the equation: time, and with it, entropy. The deactivation or poor activation of certain circuits, if for no other reason than to make sure that the ideal of goodness does not put 'a positive premium on being bad'.

We must realize that the ideal proposed by Jesus does not contain *time* in its specifications. The appointed 'time-span' of efficacy does not exist in the adventure of gratuitousness. So when Jesus faces up to the time-span of his project, he cannot employ or reckon on any quantity of time and energy whatsoever: e.g., attempting to convince his enemies as individuals or groups.

If we introduce this note of *haste and urgency*, we will begin to understand the means that Jesus actually used to deal with his enemies—especially if we consider *the long length of time* taken up by his disciples (see Mk 4:34). We will realize that he did not have time to engage in persuasion and dialogue with his adversaries. Indeed on two occasions Matthew tells us simply that Jesus just walked away from them in a huff.[169]

We will also begin to understand why he described his enemies as he did, and why he reduced them to nothing but enemies. His struggle for the kingdom, like any human struggle, was a race against the clock. Jesus treated them as if it were not worth wasting time and energy on them. That cannot help but come as a surprise to those who talk about 'sweet', 'gentle' Jesus of Nazareth, who strongly condemned any and all insults to one's brothers (Mt 5:22). For we find him doing that *ad nauseam*.[170]

A christology from above finds it easy enough to evade this problem. Jesus' use of insults is depicted as a dispassionate divine judgment, and thereby stripped of its 'sinful' character. We then find it easy to join Jesus in his holy indignation. But remember that the person who uses insults so frequently and cuttingly is the human being Jesus. We would be going directly against his most profound teachings if we first declared him God, apart from his attitudes, and then justified in him what we would not justify in any human being.

Seen in his authentic historical context, Jesus was polemical or ambiguous because he did not *appear* as isolated from Sin and a certain kind of entropy: i.e., the kind which must incorporate time and entropy into its real-life circuit, even when it clearly perceives where the ideal of richer human relationships lies.

Jesus' overcoming of Sin is as invisible as his victory over Death will be: an object of faith rather than of verifiable experience. Only when the ultimate reality is presented to faith with the resurrection, will the whole transcendent datum of Jesus' victory over Sin fit into it. Not to deny history but to make it clear that he overcomes Sin insofar as his freedom never agrees, in bad faith, to be in complicity with an entropy greater than that required for the efficacy of his history project.

•

What general conclusions might we draw from the above reflections to mark out the lines of a sounder and deeper interpretation of Jesus of Nazareth? Two, I think.

(1). Any concrete version attempting to continue the project of God's kingdom along Jesus' lines must reject idealistic purism. It must not imagine, in the name of ever unrealizable utopias, that the freer it is of ideologies the closer it is to Jesus. Such a claim is not mistaken or deluded when it says that partiality is characteristic of every ideology,[171] and that such partiality is an objectively sinful refusal to integrate all human beings into the circuit in a richer way. But it is mistaken and deluded when it sacrifices every concrete realization or achievement to a vaunted higher one, condemning their means as partial, and waiting for one that will be a faithful copy of Jesus' own faith. Because the faith of Jesus himself, as we just have seen, was fleshed out in a limited, imperfect ideology vis-à-vis the criteria he himself taught. That is the price and meaning of the incarnation.

(2). This has to do with the opposite side of the coin. The more a community, just as that which follows Jesus, tries to avoid Death by quantitative increases that seem to transcend conflicts, the more the very mechanism of the real world threatens its life and Sin enters it. For that approach attacks the very roots of its meaning, turning it into an ideology in the unwitting service of the very values opposed to those of Jesus.

Jesus kept control over his use of mass means (cheap energy) for the kingdom. The proof lies in the fact that in his death he experienced the whole energy cost of the difficult synthesis he was proposing. If the community that claims to follow him does not understand that dialectic, if it tries to justify the means it uses for its own survival and growth by saying that they are not ideological, then entropy will be uncontrollable and will become an intrinsic factor of death.

Thus keeping 'the people' within the institutional limits of the community becomes an ideological substitute that leaves those same people defenceless against the attacks they suffer. It also becomes a negative judgment on many things that should be viewed differently. By avoiding the whole dilemma of efficacy, it fails to recognize and endorse all that the risen and resurrected Jesus has caused to sprout in the world under many different forms: i.e., that fundamental partiality for every human being still deprived of its basic humanity.

CHAPTER IV

Jesus and the Recapitulation
of the Universe

The previous chapters have shown us a human being, Jesus of Nazareth, situated at a specific and crucial point in the process of universal evolution by virtue of his life and message. The values he proclaimed and urged people to hope for dovetail with the line of growing negentropy that is one of the parameters of evolution.

We have also seen that the concrete Jesus does not fit in with the theological images of an immobilized or idealized Jesus. As is true of the entire evolutionary process, he and his work adapted to the other parameter, entropy. Thus his life and message preserved the supreme evolutionary quality: flexibility.

If all that is true, then Jesus represented one of those privileged moments in which evolution bends back on itself to become conscious, hence to become a human task.

In trying to *interpret* this historical Jesus during the course of my investigation, I have tried to stay with an epistemology that comes closer to that used successfully by science in its study of evolution.[172] But that raises some questions for us: Why look to Jesus of Nazareth as the central point of meaning for that universal process, which continues after him? Why wager everything on him despite his limitations, which are evident in his concrete historical activity even though it fitted into the parameters of evolution? In short, why are we exercising anthropological faith to take Jesus out of his specific historical situation and project him back to the beginning of the universe and, even more, forward toward its end? To use New Testament language, why are we making him the Alpha and Omega of the process in which he, through humanity in its final stage, will lead everything to its definitive culmination?

This chapter will try to answer those questions and a few others associated with them.

I

We have reached the point where I must point up differences between my reflections and those of Teilhard de Chardin, who was a pioneer in this general

93

line of thought. Otherwise readers might be a bit confused, since I have used some of his ideas and intuitions in trying to frame Jesus of Nazareth in the categories of evolution.

Bateson is right when he says that thinking about the evolutionary process requires an *epistemological* change, even if we are thinking only about the biosphere and how to make an ecological contribution to it. In other words, there must be a change in the very procedure of scientific investigation.

It is not a matter of some 'discovery' that can be made by science. That can be made, and usually is, within the prevailing epistemology. What does happen, however, is that important scientific discoveries soon prompt people to modify their very mode of investigation. Physics would not be the same after Newton, yet he did not discover or utilize a new epistemology. He discovered the law of universal gravitation.

Actually few scientists draw the epistemological conclusions warranted by their own discoveries. They do not ordinarily perceive that their discovery logically calls for a new way of investigating things. I might also note that if they did, it probably would not add to their scientific reputation, at least in the short run, or help to win acceptance for their discovery. Those who move from one plane to the other are readily regarded as 'ideologues' and acclaimed by 'enthusiasts'. That happened in the last century with Freud and Marx, for example.

Freud is one typical case of the process. He began his investigations with the methods that were considered scientific in his time for the treatment of psychic illnesses. But what he discovered in the scientific field gradually induced him to create what he would call 'psychoanalysis' or 'metapsychology', to transform the way of conceiving and investigating psychic phenomena.[173]

I mention these examples only to point up the naïve confidence with which Teilhard de Chardin claims that the mechanisms of evolution constitute a 'phenomenon': i.e., something that can be established and proved scientifically, without a change of epistemology. I think that attentive readers of his work can readily see that his conclusions go considerably beyond what current science can conclude from its methods of observation. They presuppose a new method or approach for scientific investigation itself.[174]

There are two main indications of this fact. One is Teilhard's claim that he is not describing anything more than the 'phenomenon' accessible to science. The other has to do with the conclusions he draws from ordinary epistemology, apparently not considering the changes his own thinking and discoveries should have introduced into that epistemology. Let us examine these two points.

(1). In his Foreword to *The Phenomenon of Man,* Teilhard explains the reason for his title: ". . . to assert that man, in nature, is a genuine fact falling (at least partially) within the scope and the requirements and methods of science . . . I repeat that my only aim in these pages . . . is to *see*; that is to say, to develop a *homogeneous* and *coherent* perspective of our general extended experience of man . . . "[175] Again stressing the 'scientific' as opposed to metaphysical character of his work and its content, he writes: "The true physics is that which will, one day, achieve the inclusion of man in his wholeness in a coherent picture of the world."[176]

But Teilhard does not seem to notice when his thought adds *transcendent data* to the experiential data that can properly be called scientific. He does not seem to notice when he moves from datum to interpretation and infers a datum that in itself is unverifiable and hence not scientific. This is true of many scientists, of course; but it is all the clearer in his case insofar as his thought soars higher and embraces more.

Let me just give one example here, to which we will have to return later in this chapter. Teilhard has shown the consequences of the laws of thermodynamics. Here I leave aside the question whether the latter are verifiable objective data in all their extension, and focus on the consequences themselves.

The most important is that the undeniable progressive realization of negentropy is not, properly speaking, a 'victory' over entropy. As we saw, 'Maxwell's demon', the invisible creator of negentropy, also consumes energy. The activity of all the agents of negentropy, then, does not interrupt or invalidate the process leading energy to ever more degraded and unusable forms.

Another important fact here is that the successes of negentropy have a short life. Along the lines of Bateson in his metalogue, Teilhard writes: "Little by little, the *improbable* combinations that they represent become broken down again into more simple components, which fall back and are disaggregated in the shapelessness of *probable* distributions."

What conclusion is to be drawn from that? Teilhard does not hesitate: "A rocket rising in the wake of time's arrow, that only bursts to be extinguished; an eddy rising on the bosom of a descending current—such then must be . . . [the figure] of the world. So says science: and I believe in science: but up to now has science ever troubled to look at the world other than from *without*?"[177] What follows next is a chapter entitled 'The Within of Things'. But what is his 'within' if not an unverifiable extrapolation of that which is observed in beings endowed with a nervous system and hence consciousness? How can Teilhard continue to call that a 'phenomenon'?

Gregory Bateson is right when he writes that the epistemological premises people use to structure their experience and life become at least partially *self-validating* for the person in question.[178] A person chooses the premises and then continues to punctuate sequences of events accordingly. Now one might imagine that Jacques Monod would disagree, given his conception of science. But that is not the case, at least in principle. Monod's 'postulate of objectivity' does not flow from facts or statistics. It is no more nor less than a wager or a 'self-validating premise'. Near the very end of *Chance and Necessity* he writes:

This prohibition, this 'first commandment' which ensures the foundation of objective knowledge, is not itself objective. It cannot be objective: it is an ethical guideline, a rule for conduct. True knowledge is ignorant of values, but it cannot be grounded elsewhere than upon a value judgment, or rather upon an *axiomatic* value.[179]

This is clearly what Bateson considers the choosing of an epistemological premise. And it should be obvious from what Monod says next that this premise, arbitrarily chosen, is or becomes self-validating:

> It is obvious that the positing of the principle of objectivity as the condition of true knowledge *constitutes an ethical choice and not a judgment arrived at from knowledge, since, according to the postulate's own terms, there cannot have been any 'true' knowledge prior to this arbitral choice.* In order to establish the *norm* for knowledge the objectivity principle defines a *value*: that value is objective knowledge itself. Thus, assenting to the principle of objectivity one announces one's adherence to the basic statement of an ethical system, one asserts the ethic of knowledge.[180]

It cannot be otherwise. We have here a wager generalized to the whole field of knowledge and grounded in an 'ought' or value that the person prefers to others. It is futile to claim, as does Teilhard de Chardin, that we are dealing with a 'phenomenon', with something dictated by reality itself. The most we can say is that we are dealing with a datum inferred from the way things usually present themselves to us and intimately bound up with the values we have chosen. As our 'premise', it will be a part of our every act of cognition, carrying it in a direction that transcends any and all concrete experience from the start, giving form to it, and linking it up with others. For that very reason, the person who chooses that 'premise' (on the basis of a certain value) *knows* its consequences. And Monod does not hide the fact:

> It is perfectly true that science outrages values. Not directly, since science is no judge of them and *must* ignore them; but it subverts every one of the mythical or philosophical ontogenies upon which the animist[181] tradition, from the Australian aborigines to the dialectical materialists, has made all ethics rest: values, duties, rights, prohibitions. If he accepts this message—accepts all it contains—then man must at last wake out of his millenary dream; and in doing so, wake to his total solitude, his fundamental isolation. Now does he at last realize that, like a gypsy, he lives on the boundary of an alien world. A world that is deaf to his music, just as indifferent to his hopes as it is to his suffering or his crimes.[182]

Now if this premise does become self-*validating,* as Monod admits, what are we to say about the knowledge or realization Monod alludes to in the second, last sentence just cited? It might seem to be a 'phenomenon' that leaps to our eyes, but of course it is not. Does that mean it is beyond any criterion of evaluation, that it is 'indisputable' in the strictest sense of the word? I think it is 'indisputable' in that sense, but I also think it can be evaluated. This evaluation can only be indirect, but it is nevertheless crucial: To what extent can a human being *coherently* structure the whole realm of knowledge and ultimately his or her whole (ethical) behavior around that basic premise?

As we saw in an earlier chapter, the very hypotheses that Monod regards as 'scientific' do not conform *logically* to that premise. As if that were not enough, Monod says it is a question of value (see page 96 above). But what *value* could there be in a discipline devoted to explaining a world that is alien to humanity and meaningless for it?[183] I will let my readers pass their own judgment on the issue, since I am not concerned with Monod's thought here. Instead I wish to focus on the opposite view that we have been discussing. What transcendent data are implied in the opposite wager, the bet on the final victory of negentropy and meaningfulness? Which is another way of asking: On what bases or premises does an ecology of mind and the world rest?

That brings us back to what Teilhard calls 'the within' of things. Only instead of pretending it is a 'phenomenon', we now see it as a logical exigency of an epistemological premise that has been deliberately chosen and elaborated in place of Monod's. It is *a way of seeing* the universe, from which will also issue a way of transforming the universe in line with *all* its possibilities and all the values that can be extracted from it.

Recall Teilhard's description of 'the figure' of the world (see p. 95). Instead of 'figure' or 'picture', we might more correctly use the word 'phenomenon'.[184] We may now ask: Is there something *behind* or *within* that phenomenon? Is there some datum *transcending* the visible and verifiable aspect of it (e.g., the 'big numbers' of statistics) that can give greater *logical* coherence to Teilhard's talk about 'the within' of things, about a hidden dimension that will lead them to the Omega point, which is somehow identified with Jesus in his cosmic dimensions?

(2). That brings us to the second point. I suggested that Teilhard claims to found a new epistemology, but manages to do so only partially. And, in my opinion, this is due to the fact that his thinking remains linear to a large extent. In other words, he moves too quickly from the ideal to its realization. I would almost go so far as to say that he is a crypto-Lamarckian, even though he writes explicitly about the role of entropy and chance.[185]

One support for my view is the problem posed by what Teilhard calls the 'Omega point' of evolution. It is the goal of evolution, present and operative from the very beginning. The problem, I would suggest, is that his 'Omega point' is the 'linear' realization of *one* of the forms taken by energy in the process of evolution. It is *negentropy* carried to the point of complete *liberation* from every entropic tendency. And we have already seen what happens when a line of thought refuses to integrate the element of entropy into the circuit of efficacy.

On the one hand the 'exterior' figure of the world is not one of solid progress toward Omega, as Teilhard himself suggests. Even though directed toward Omega, it is slowing down and moving toward exhaustion and immobility because of a lack of usable energy. That is why Teilhard moves on to discuss the 'within' of things, which purports to be the other side of the picture. But since this growing 'within' is equivalent to negentropy, which is already present in the 'without' of things, it is not surprising that Teilhard ends his new chapter with these unanswered questions:

> Is this final and resultant form of radial energies,[186] supposing it exists, subject to reversal? Is it destined one day to start disintegrating so as to satisfy the principle of entropy, and fall back indefinitely into pre-living and still lower centres, by the exhaustion and levelling-down of the free tangential energy contained in the successive envelopes of the universe from which it has emerged?[187]

I suggest, then, that Teilhard's recourse to a linear logic prevented him from giving coherence or plausibility to his 'Omega point' in a world where entropy, *in time,* has the last word.[188] The problem is that Teilhard did not really take full note of his epistemological premise, of the fact that it included an anthropological faith and was not just a matter of seeing the phenomenon. For that premise should have led him at this point to explore the whole theme of *resurrection* that goes by way of death and seems to be such.

II

To talk about resurrection, either the personal one of Jesus or the universal one at the end of history, is obviously to introduce a *transcendent datum.* As we saw in Volume II, the gospel accounts suggest that the paschal experiences of Jesus' disciples in meeting him can have only one meaning. They are an initial peek at the ultimate and definitive world, at what theology describes as the *eschatological* reality. That is the wager: that *in the end* the values which showed up in Jesus' historical project will dominate reality as a whole; that the 'ought-to-be' contained in them will turn out to be. But we must remember the price: the abolition of time, and hence of history and entropy.

Is such a wager reasonable and meaningful today, in a world dominated by science? Wouldn't it be falling back into the millenarian dream, the "animism" scorned by Monod, which tries to bend the universe to the values that human freedom decides to realize?

Let me be clear about what I am going to do here. I have been operating with an epistemological premise: i.e., the overall analogy of the universe, whether it be due to the redundancy of nature or the structure of the human mind. Now I am going to ask two questions that seem perfectly reasonable and that cannot be justifiably avoided: (1) Does the transcendent datum just discussed above fit in more logically with my epistemological premise than does the opposite transcendent datum; if the answer is yes, (2) how can that 'datum' about the definitive future take place without contradicting the other data that we are shown by the world as we know it?

(1). As we saw in the previous section, the epistemological premise opposed to global analogy and anthropomorphism banishes values from the universe. The world is assembled and disassembled according to laws that are deaf to the virtues and crimes of human beings. It offers no meaning to freedom, which thus shows up in all its radical and crucial foreignness.[189]

The epistemological premise presented by Bateson as his own is, in principle, the opposite. The world, whose evolution seems to begin without meaning, is nevertheless a 'mind' that surfaces gradually and then takes over the reins of the entire evolutionary process. *Meaning,* which hardly seemed to exist at all in the primordial mechanisms, becomes decisive in the most developed, i.e., the latest, products of evolution. Thus a 'mind' is *ecological* when it maintains the necessary balance (or flexibility) between its projects (its 'intentionality') and its respect for the energy mechanisms of the environment; when it maintains the optimal circuit equation between meaning and realism, negentropy and entropy.

The first thing that seems to be demanded by this flexible equilibrium, on which natural and mental ecology is based, is a certain *modesty* in our desire for meaning, in our human pretensions. We should accustom ourselves to the irremediable limitation of meaningfulness, in order to avoid those escalations of means that inevitably end up destroying meaning in the name of realizing it.

It is sane and healthy[190] to reproduce in our mind the process by which nature obtains its objectives. In doing that, we cannot forget the 'positive side' of death.[191] Indeed we cannot forget how necessary it is if, in a world of limited, constant energy, new beings are to face up to the problems of meaning with better possibilities.

Bateson rightly stresses the risk we run when we try to evade this necessity with infantile subterfuges: "In order to escape the million metaphoric deaths depicted in a universe of *circles* of causation, we are eager to deny the simple reality of ordinary dying and to build fantasies of an afterworld and even of reincarnation."[192]

Now I would like to note a few things here. *In the first place,*[193] there is here a major misunderstanding or mistake about the motivations for human action deriving from the individual on the one hand and from the species on the other.

It is quite possible that my own way of expressing myself in this volume has contributed to this misunderstanding. I have suggested that in its ultimate stage evolution becomes a task for the human being—meaning the human species. It will depend on all human beings as a group whether the evolutionary process continues to go forward on the wings of flexibility, or becomes increasingly inflexible and ends up in a catastrophe engulfing all.

But now we note something that is very curious at every glance. Evolution, which has prepared humanity as a *species* for this task, has not endowed each human *individual* with a direct interest in the species. Each human being begins the adventure of life as if it were the center of the universe. It refers everything to itself, and from its own standpoint it structures its existence around values that have been chosen from the many that the human species displays in the showcase of its memory.

Thus evolution does not turn Lamarckian when it arrives at the human level. Its ultimate creation, the responsible human, creates *centers.* Nature, which up to then seemed to be one, explodes into as many centers as there are individual freedoms, which it of course has managed to bring into being.

Now these *centers,* precisely as centers, are *the most unpredictable* thing imaginable in relation to their species, whether or not you accept the thesis that the human being enjoys real freedom. At the human level nature goes in for redundancy, re-creating the needed slowness and reintroducing *chance* in a different form: i.e., that of the individual, who will integrate the interests of the species into its projects only by diverse, difficult, and indirect journeyings.

Here, once again, we see the 'Weissmann barrier' giving new balance and flexibility to the evolutionary process. Counteracting the suicidal pretentions of the Lamarckian hypothesis, Weissmann stressed the necessity of a barrier between somatic change and the genetic code.[194] And in our case here, it means that the human individual is not structured in terms of the species.

I hope it is obvious that my remarks are not meant to be a panegryic to individualism. Still less am I trying to claim that each human being chooses its path to happiness in solitude. As we saw in the early chapters of Volume I (*Faith and Ideologies*), only the memory of the species offers each individual, within structured social limits, the witnesses in whom it can place the faith required for its existential wager.

What I *am* saying here is that the barrier just noted above makes it impossible to satisfy the need for meaningfulness in any human activity with some invisible species-result. Such activity must simultaneously show up as the realization or fulfillment of the *person,* if it is to dynamize all the energies of the individual.[195] And I mean 'dynamize' in the strict sense of the word.

To put it another way and in summary fashion, the human person has to throw an inauthentic veil over its own death (as Heidegger suggested in *Being and Time*). We wait on the death of others and turn our backs on our own, so that we can work *as if* our own death did not doom our projects to uselessness. To substitute the finality or purpose of the species for that of the individual is to indulge in a confusion of logical levels.

In the second place, we must remember that it is easy enough for human beings to go into the world of meaning and sense; the hard part for them is coming out of it. The realm of meaning and values entails the renunciation of measurements, especially temporal measurements. The demands of meaningfulness are 'quantum' demands, and the 'quantity' in question is nothing more nor less than the 'totality'.

Let's take an example for the world of art.[196] I give you a sculptor whose only raw material is quite perishable. In a few years the raw material will give out and that will be the end of his sculpture. What is the sculptor to do? You answer: feeling a vocation to create beauty, the sculptor will work with that perishable material.

But suppose the 'corruption' of the raw material goes even faster; that while he or she is sculpting one part, the other parts are already falling apart and perishing; that our sculptor will never actually see the statue he or she wanted to make. If the work can never be seen or recognized as such by its maker, will our sculptor keep on with the work?

In short, what temporal limit or measurement of durability will keep meaningfulness alive? Two or three days? A century? It is possible that two days might suffice, *provided that* the difficulties entailed in doing the work are not too great. Otherwise it would not be worth the trouble; it would not make sense. For the sake of meaning, you see, the human being has the strange capacity and need to eternalize the values on which it wagers. Its feverish imagination creates multitudes who will recognize and appreciate its work of art, however ephemeral it may be, for centuries to come. This is the capacity and need, of which I was speaking, to live and act in despite of death—one's own and that of the universe.

In itself meaning does not know time. Two people who are truly in love with each other will pronounce the word 'forever'. If they do not, they will not give themselves to each other intimately; they will use each other as instruments and conclude that it did not make sense, that it was not worth the trouble.

Meaning and value are equivalent words; both are a wager on the definitive. But if the latter is spirited away by some trickery, even if it be in the name of heaven, then the former vanishes as well. No one has pointed this out better than Teilhard de Chardin, a Christian, with a rhetorical question that many might find scandalous: "What does it matter to us to be rewarded in heaven if, in the final reckoning, we have not added *one iota of absolute* to the totality of being through our lives?"[197]

This rhetorical question would be pretentious if we disregarded evolution and chose to consider human beings solely in terms of their brief, ephemeral existence on earth. But it takes on profound and logical urgency when we consider how the way has gradually been paved for this goal and font of meaning: each individual human being.

In the third place, then, we see that if order is the first thing, a 'mind' had to be present from the very start of the universe. The very first element of negentropy to appear in the primordial realm was already dependent on that mind and arose out of it. At that level mind was *one* and unique, capable of 'catching' chance in its most varied forms and also of waiting for and utilizing all that is signified in the concentration and complexity of energy.

With regard to this 'mind', which has been ordering the universe and drawing it out of the chaos of pure chance for an unfathomable length of time, Bateson rightly hints that it could be called *God*.[198] He is not trying to prove the existence of an infinite being apart from the world, nor is he postulating some sort of pantheism. The point simply is that whatever content we may give to the word 'God', it must somehow coincide with the mind that uses chance to create order and meaning.

Now what shows up rather surprisingly in evolution is the fact that in its latest stages this mind manages to create, not order directly, but 'minds' endowed with the ability and the need to create order. And to say order is to say meaning.

If reality as a whole had not obeyed that global mind, the appearance of meaning would not have been possible. But it is equally incomprehensible that this final stage of order, in which many minds join in the task of creating meaning, would be doomed to constant failure; that values would systematically crumble in exhaustion as they sought to be transformed into reality. In that case the mind that began the operation of meaning, the absolute itself, would be nothing more than what Teilhard described as 'an eddy rising on the bosom of a descending current' (see p. 95 above). And that would represent an incomprehensible contradiction.

With this whole set of reflections I have not been trying to *prove* anything. I simply wanted to break down some of the defence mechanisms embodied in certain misunderstanding of language and imagination. My aim was to show that the transcendent datum regarding the victory of meaning over Death, the latter being the symbol and sign of definitive unfulfillment—is not illusion or the product of a credulous mind. Instead it flows from something that is thoroughly and profoundly consistent with basic human dimensions. As such, it is a reasonable wager to which Jesus is a privileged witness.

(2). But can we envision and think about such a victory without falling into infantile contradictions, escapisms, or myths that no scientific thinking can logically accept? We certainly are not going to ask science to accept something it cannot verify. When I talk about something it cannot logically accept here, I am referring to things that would contradict the mechanisms that the various sciences discover in the verifiable plane. Something 'contradictory' is not simply something 'different'.

The transcendent data offered by the Bible are certainly 'different'. The biblical authors of both Testaments did not possess the categories we can use today. So we can only expect them to offer a vague approximation, in largely iconic language, to this transcendent datum about eschatological reality. In short, we can only expect them to provide a 'mythic' description. But remember that mythical language must be interpreted, not suppressed. It is not an erroneous language. It is a primordial language in code.

In the New Testament we come across four main terms that are used to describe the final reality: resurrection, regeneration, restoration, and recapitulation. All of them, except the term 'resurrection', are used only once or twice in the whole New Testament; but they occupy central places. The first, 'resurrection' *(anastasis)*, is used abundantly. That is not surprising since it was a religious concept current in Jesus' day and even before that. Indeed the religious context of Jesus' time was divided precisely around that notion. The Sadducees denied there was any resurrection (Mt 22:23), whereas the Pharisees believed in it.

Nevertheless the term retains its importance for our question here. Not too long before the Christian era, this world was the only existential horizon for human beings of the Old Testament. Whence the idea of 'standing up' again after death? It came from a need for *meaning*. As we see in Job, Ecclesiastes,

and many Psalms, people noted that there was no relationship between historical happenings and the moral caliber of human beings, as they had once
believed there was. So their present, verifiable world seemed increasingly
inadequate in terms of meaning and sense.

The idea that creation (or providence) operates in total disregard of the
meaning that human beings are trying to put into their activity, so as to make
their life meaningful, defies all logic or coherence. It was necessary to widen
the temporal span in order to find a place for that meaning. It was less
improbable to envision a life beyond death, where people would be treated in
accordance with the quality of their work, than to envision a creation that put
an irrevocable end to a person's existence with physical death.

As we saw in Volume III to some extent, and will see again here, Paul will
give much more human depth to this transcendent datum. Basically he stripped
it of its purely individual cast, wherein the 'other life' was designed to judge,
reward, or punish each individual human being.

Before we get into that, let us recall something else in connection with the
two terms 'regeneration' (*palingenesis*) and 'restoration' (*apokatastasis*).
From the very start of the Old Testament there was a vague feeling that creation
(or the universe, if you prefer), as it was operating, could not be the one that
had issued in pristine perfection from the creative word of God. What we
would call 'entropy' today was sometimes attributed to some first human sin,
sometimes to rebel angels. That is not unusual, since people living in a fixist
context could not envision any other alternatives. Very gradually, however,
biblical humanity began to discover the transcendent characteristics of the
creation of the universe in all their radicalness, and with that the immense
power of what we today would call 'negentropy' to place all the energy of the
cosmos in the service of meaning. So the victory of the individual over death
began to take on broader dimensions, coming to be identified with a *new
creation* (Rev 21:1–5). In his major letters Paul himself suggests that the
datum manifested in Jesus' resurrection is something so new that it amounts
to a new creation of the human being and all that surrounds it (2 Cor 5:17;
Gal 5:15).[199]

At the end of the Book of Revelation, however, the theme of the new
creation (or regeneration, or universal restoration) acquires important shad-
ings. The One who with apparent effortlessness was able to create a first earth,
where meaning made its way painfully only to be corrupted later, is not going to
offer the compensation or reward of a 'heaven', of a world different from the
one where human meaning and values were so laboriously sought after.

In the 'new creation' it is a *new earth* that the Creator is preparing for
humanity. This is an eloquent indication that humanity is not to be rewarded, in
a different world, for the sufferings of this earth. But of course the new earth
will be 'different'. The old curse that condemned the earth to entropy will no
longer exist (Rev 22:3). God "will wipe away every tear from their eyes, and
death shall be no more, neither shall there be mourning nor crying nor pain any
more, for the old world has passed away" (Rev 21:4).

There are two further elements of major importance, quite aside from the fact that 'new earth' suggests the transposition of our earthly existence to another in which all the things that seemed to negate our values and our efforts to implant them in this existence are done away with. One element is the allusion to some sort of filter being placed between what was realized on the first earth and what will form part of the second, definitive earth (Rev 21:26–27).[200]

The second element is profoundly christological. And it is not surprising that christologies 'from above' systematically disregard it, for it seems to diminish God if we think of God apart from Jesus. The 'new earth' is 'the new heaven' of God (Rev 21:1). In other words, God locates his new and definitive dwelling there where the values of the human being, now liberated, flourish in full bloom. Thus the meaning of history, in which humanity takes part and struggles, is not going to be replaced by something else; it is going to be absolutized in the new, definitive creation. God is not presented as a spectator of the human struggle for meaning. Instead God is identified with its culmination.

That brings us to a consideration of the fourth term: 'recapitulation' (*anakephalaiosis*). The term shows up in a central text of New Testament christology: the hymn to Jesus in Ephesians 1:3–14. It also shows up in a central passage of Paul dealing with Christian morality and the complete fulfillment of the Law. That Pauline passage is no less christological than the hymn in Ephesians, particularly when we examine it in terms of the categories elaborated here in Volume V.

We already know from Volume III (*The Humanist Christology of Paul*) that the real, deeper meaning of the term 'to recapitulate' (to 'put a head on') is 'to give meaning' to something. It is in that sense that different things are brought together in unity and given culmination. Now the Pauline ethical text reflects, point by point, the law of evolution spelled out by Vatican II with regard to negentropy or love. And all the mechanisms or laws of the universe, including ethical ones, 'aspire' to this same goal: "Have no debt with anyone except that of mutual love. The one who loves neighbor has fulfilled the Law. You see. . . all the other precepts are recapitulated ['acquire meaning'] in this formula [*logos* or norm]: 'You shall love your neighbor as yourself'. . . Hence love is the Law in its fullness" (Rom 13:8–10).

But the divided human being whom Paul analyzes in Romans 7 does not seem able to confer that meaning on its performances, though it yearns to do so. It is like our imaginary sculptor. Entropy seems to disintegrate the material into which the human being seeks to implant its ideal, even as we handle the 'instruments' for its realization. Thus the universe seems condemned to uselessness (Rom 8:20), to meaninglessness and headlessness.

Or is it possible that this is merely one side of history, the deceptive side that humanity can see? Is there another hidden side? That is precisely what the author of the Letter to the Ephesians suggests when he writes that God's plan is to 'recapitulate' in Christ all things in heaven and on earth (Eph 1:10).

Note how this dovetails with what we saw in Revelation 21:1. Even celestial reality makes no sense unless human beings and their freedom can introduce into the definitive reality something of the love they carry as an aspiration in their inner humanity (Rom 7:22). God coincides with the meaning of human work.

That is why the theme of 'resurrection' is shifted by Paul from the revivification of the individual to the 'manifestation' (*apokalupsis*) and 'glory' of the *freedom* of God's children (Rom 8:19, 21).

Hence it is not a matter of some necessity imposed by the old scenario of judgment. Or it is a judgment, if you prefer, in the sense that the false visible aspect of what we are building for the definitive with our work will be replaced by a correct and manifest estimation of the quality and value of each person's work (1 Cor 3:13). Not to mete out rewards or punishments, but to determine whether that work or part of it is to have a place in the new and definitive earth.

As *manifestation,* resurrection does not so much suggest a 'second creation' as an opening up to the true vision, an *epistemological conversion.* We gain access to a vision liberated from time, entropy, and the deceiving impact of 'big numbers'. We come to discover the true ties of causality that were built up in the order of meaning, but that are invisible now because of the ongoing deactivations that are needed.

Certain mysterious 'resurrections' already seem to be harbingers of the new vision, which we are to incorporate now as a new way of punctuating the flow of events. Paul alludes to the resurrection of meaningfulness[201] when one's own autonomy is submitted to death and chance: the seed that dies and rises again, unrecognizable, in a plant, the latter being different from the seed that was sown and disappeared. When we look at evolution in vague, overall terms, we see the victorious resurrection of a growing negentropy after every deactivation, though the forms may be vague and confusing. The inevitable deactivations are precisely the thing that renders the causality impenetrable and anonymous in a world of entropy. When the category of *time* is abolished, along with the logical necessity it entails of always handing over the result of our effort to impersonal chance,[202] our effort will show up for the deeper reality it was: something united with the source of its existence in the human and divine project that is the continuation of Jesus' own project.

Thus the glance that humanity casts at evolution as a whole from the artificial endpoint of today is logically connected in meaning with the image that Paul offers us of creation when it has arrived at the true and definitive *today* and hence been restored to the consciousness of all those human beings who wagered on it and imprinted values and meaning on it.

III

What, then, is this *Omega* or goal of the universe? Contrary to what Teilhard de Chardin seems to claim, it is not the point where the energies present in the 'phenomenon' of evolution converge. If by 'phenomenon' he means something that we need only open our eyes to see and verify, something that does not call for interpretation or extrapolation, then Jesus-Omega is not that universal phenomenon. It is a *transcendent datum that is grounded in faith,* be it religious or anthropological, and that in turn grounds the reasonableness of that faith.

Here again I am talking about the faith I discussed in Volume I (*Faith and Ideologies*). Up to this point it is anthropological faith, which every human being uses as the basis for its existential wager and its structuring of a world of meaning. This faith *always* implies transcendent data, which are more or less positive or negative. These 'premises' are accepted for their own worth (on the basis of witnesses on their behalf who guarantee them). They then are 'verified' existentially insofar as they fit in logically and coherently with the other data that the human being perceives and with the values it desires to realize.

Seen from that standpoint, it is just as transcendent for Monod to imagine a world deaf to the human being and its music, or indifferent to its hopes, sufferings, and crimes,[203] as it is for us to imagine it guided by a love that cannot fail toward the new earth, one which will have room only for the negentropy that has been slowly and painfully elaborated by God and the human beings who are God's collaborators (*synergoi*).

But it should be noted that these collaborators are all human beings of good will.[204] Teilhard de Chardin doesn't deny that directly, but he does seem to deny it indirectly. How? By positing the Omega point in a 'linear' continuation of pure negentropy, he prematurely deifies *the Church* along with Jesus.[205]

I indicated earlier that this 'linear' tendency usually minimizes the need that Jesus had, as a completely human being, to integrate entropy into his circuit. From the most reliable historical witnesses we have to him and his work, on the other hand, we learn that Jesus did indeed integrate entropy into his circuit.

So we find two contrasting things here. On the one hand the historical Jesus is in the *total* line or course of evolution because he combined negentropy and entropy in the richest way he could. On the other hand a Church that dehistoricizes Jesus because it views him as God will always be tempted to identify itself with *only one* of the lines of evolution: negentropy. Hence it will be without basis or efficacy. So while the historical Jesus was an agent of the evolutionary quality par excellence, *flexibility,* the Church often has appeared to be, even today, an agent and embodiment of the opposite, idealistic factor: inflexibility.

This means that the lesson taught by evolution must be repeated again for the community that claims to follow and continue Jesus. Imbalance is produced when the needed dose of entropy is not integrated into the quest for results in the order of meaning and values; and this imbalance leads to something that is counterproductive. It leads to an increase of entropy, which unexpectedly turns those values into something anti-evolutionary. Resisting death only produces the fruits of death.

That is precisely what happens when the religious faith invested in Jesus resists the hazardous but inevitable immersion in history that takes place through limited, contingent ideologies. For the sake of the purity of the faith, it waits and hopes for some fully Christian type of efficacy (ideology) to take up the full meaning and value of the Christian message and implant it as such in reality. Or, and this comes down to the same thing, it waits and hopes for human beings to grow tired of their ill will and finally bow, of their own accord, to the 'Christian' solutions.

This unleashes entropy in two ways, both embodied in inflexibility. On the one hand the community of Jesus is deprived of any realistic historical commitment, even to the lesser evil, by virtue of its idealism. It thus becomes the false refuge of those who adhere only to the Christian 'religion', looking to it for a mistaken and inoperative system of efficacy (i.e., an ideology) and hence leaving the field of history open to the forces of the *status quo*.

On the other hand the Christian community continues to shape itself as a mass, and it is typical of the mass to think in 'linear' terms. Which means it cannot recognize the forms that have passed through death and resurrection to bring the values of Jesus to fruition in the most unexpected and disconcerting ways. There is really no point in a minority of that Church trying to recognize them if that minority is discredited by the vast majority, who can see and recognize the Christian reality only in what is Christian. When chance, 'caught on the wing', brings these new forms to the surface, it often strips them of any and all *appearances of continuity,* which are the only kind that can be readily and 'linearly' recognized as deriving from Jesus.

Like Jesus, you see, his community must die and rise day after day. The death is visible, the resurrection is not. There is a wager involved, which only faith can make. Only thus will Jesus continue to be a factor of flexibility for a humanity that holds in its hands the future evolution of the world. Only thus will the latter get as close as possible to that Omega point that is its horizon.

CHAPTER V

By Way of Conclusion

Why put a final period here to the search I began in this volume and try to draw a few conclusions? For many reasons, which I hope my readers will understand and appreciate.

The first has to do with any study of the problem we are dealing with here, and I did allude to it in the Introduction. But here may be the place to stress again one new and surprising aspect of the enterprise we have undertaken.

That aspect is the very notion of *context*. To mention only two efforts at christological creation that have been examined in these volumes, that of Paul for the cultural world of his time (Volume III) and that of Ignatius Loyola for his cultural world in the sixteenth century (Volume IV), we find that their contexts were *given* in both cases. They were obvious conditioning factors, well-trodden roads, imposed and necessary categories from which no escape was possible, partly because they were not even consciously noted as such. It was only 'natural' for certain categories and sets of problems to be incorporated into their interpretation of Jesus. And that very 'naturalness' forced us to explore the underlying context, so that we would not take for granted and obvious what in fact is not.

Here in Volume V the situation is very different, if not the very opposite. On the one hand the evolutionary explanation of life, if not of matter in its totality, has made much headway and gained widespread acceptance. The world is seen as the product of a slow evolutionary process. On the other hand there is also a 'feeling of catastrophe' in the air. It seems that 'the sorcerer's apprentice' (*homo*) may cause the world to splinter into pieces with one false move at any moment. Ecology is one manifestation of this sense of catastrophe. But it is increasingly being felt in politics, economics, and other key sectors of human collective life.

For all that to form a *context*, however, there would have to be some *bridge* between the evolutionary explanation and the 'feeling of catastrophe'. That is precisely what is lacking at the moment, and what makes our 'context' so peculiar and special.

As yet we have not generalized and internalized the conviction that the 'prudence' required by our situation consists basically in 'imitating' the prudence that managed to cross all the earlier thresholds and crises, so that now at last the *power* to assume our future evolution has been left in our own hands.

The supposed *novelty* of our problems today causes us to look disdainfully, if not merely nostalgically, at the past, to see it as totally irrelevant for present-day issues. Teilhard's own image of past problems as 'problems of the hold' hint at the same sort of disdainful evaluation of the past. History has ceased to appear before us as the great 'teacher of life', precisely at the moment when we most need its teachings when viewed in all its complexity.

The most immediate consequence of all this for our task here is that Jesus is proclaimed and interpreted today, with the support of the gospel, without any regard for the human problematic that is felt to be more urgent and crucial. As if he were incompetent or irrelevant in helping us to solve it.[206]

The non-existence of the bridge in question is certainly one of the main reasons why I cannot go much further with my task, why I must content myself with a simple outline.

Another reason is closely bound up with the first. However creditable the evolutionary 'explanation' may be overall, and perhaps even *proved* by the findings of paleontology, it does not go much beyond certain general affirmations.[207] It would hardly occur to anyone to appeal to that 'explanation' as a *norm* or policy for survival and progress; and the reason is that the *large mechanisms* used systematically by the process still remain in obscurity.

It so happens that the *small mechanisms* of the process have been studied by various specialized sciences that have little connection with each other. This is not to suggest that various particular mechanisms of this sort are not known reliably or accurately in the scientific world. They are. But the successes of preciseness in different scientific disciplines easily lead to a supposedly 'scientific' opposition to any use of *loose* thinking about evolution. There is opposition to analogical, popularized, or cultural visions of evolution, or else dullness and clumsiness with regard to them.[208]

The consequences are clear and important on the plane of culture. The circulating epistemology, which should characterize our 'context', is not even *informed* about what prevails in the various natural sciences, much less able to inform the categories used in thinking about human phenomena.[209] To put it another way: an authentic evolutionary *context* does not even exist, one with categories coined by the culture and used as 'the obvious' on the plane of human culture.

This accounts for two particular features of this volume. One is my continual recourse to Gregory Bateson. After Teilhard de Chardin, and certainly with a larger dose of strict thinking, he was one of the few scientists known to me who could establish the basic supports for a bridge between our ecological urgencies (already shared by the culture) and the mechanisms in force in various, widely scattered sciences that are incomprehensible to the layman. My dependence on Bateson does not blind me to the limitations that this may entail, not only for the understanding of this section of my christological investigation today but also for its value in the future.

The second feature of this work stemming from our lack of an authentic evolutionary *context* is also peculiar. In trying to explore the meaning and significance of Jesus in our 'context' today, I have been forced to describe that context. I had to begin by spelling out the categories that should constitute it. I could not, as is usually the case, take those categories for granted as the habitual ones.

My readers will thus better appreciate and evaluate the extent of my own specific limitations, and why I end my reflection here. I am fully aware of the provisional nature of the epistemology employed (insofar as it has been elaborated up to this moment), and of my own lack of competence to judge it from the strictly scientific point of view.

There is another reason of no small importance. This seed of reflection is subject to the general law: it must die if it is to bear fruit. Others will give it more finished forms, which this author cannot calculate or even envision.

For all the above reasons, then, the 'conclusions' of Volume V amount to little more than an acknowledgement of the field that is opening before us.

I

My readers have probably noticed that I have been circling around one and the same topic from the opening pages of this volume to this point. I have made a circuit of circuits.

The circuits I have been analyzing here have been those constructed on a delicate energy calculus by the message of Jesus and that of Paul. A calculus that must be made over and over again insofar as transformations occur in the human context where such reflections take place.

It cannot be a matter of chance that the Christian tradition, viewed in terms of all its elements, has shown considerable flexibility over the twenty centuries of its existence. This is all the more surprising since its more widely broadcast version has seemed to be more inflexible, indeed a factor making for inflexibility. We saw examples of that in the final section of the previous chapter.

As we have already noted, a certain disregard for the dialectic required of any thinking that seeks to perpetuate its significance in history has often prompted people to identify the Christian with what was in fact pre-Christian. In short, there have been relapses into conceptions more akin to those attacked by Jesus than to his own. Sometimes these relapses have seemed more necessary or understandable, as when the Christian Church faced the task of civilizing the barbarian peoples of the West.[210]

The thing for me to do here, then, is to examine my conclusions in terms of those elements that seem to be the most genuine and universal in the message of Jesus. And since we have verified the radical fidelity of Paul's christological creation to that message, we shall base our comparison on the conclusions we reached in Volume III regarding Paul's thought.[211]

(1). We saw that in Paul's thought the conception of an *incomplete creation* was closely tied in with the meaningfulness of human freedom, hence of human existence overall. Indeed Paul goes so far as to talk about a universe subjected to uselessness and corruption unless human beings are capable of redeeming it with their creativity.

This conception is framed within a christological and anthropological treatment. Paul is not interested in doing a theology of *creation* as such: i.e., of God's creative work. Thus at first glance it might seem excessive or wrongheaded to attribute to Paul the thought that creation, *from the very beginning*, was deliberately left unfinished by God in order to give meaning and crucial importance to the human being and its freedom. One might be inclined to think it was Sin, introduced by Adam, that subjected the universe to corruption, uselessness, and Death.

When all is said and done, however, all that matters little—for two reasons. The *first* reason has to do with the internal logic of Paul's thought. The *second* reason has to do with the transcendent data we can add to his thought today.

With regard to the first reason, we note an important fact. As far back as the Middle Ages, there was much debate over a question that might seem abstruse and pointless to us today: *What would have happened, if Adam had not sinned?* This question was argued against the backdrop of Paul's 'gospel', the assumption being that the biblical account of Eden was historically true and that the sin of Adam had been propagated to all human beings. The problem lay in the fact that Adam, being free, could have avoided that sin, in which case there would have been no real reason or motive for the coming of Jesus, God incarnate, to redeem us from Sin and restore God's plan. Adam would have continued to live happily in Paradise, without ever feeling a need or desire for such a 'redeemer'.

The main argument against this solution was the *lack of due proportion* it entailed, particularly in the ends pursued. Was it possible that the greatest thing that had ever happened to humanity depended on a defect or failing in God's original plan, that it had not been included in that plan from the very beginning? There was also a lack of proportion in the means. The most precious thing in absolute terms—God made human being—would have been turned into a means to restore the paradisiacal existence of Adam and his progeny; and how poorly it was done![212]

Now this argument is very weighty with regard to the inner logic of Paul's thought as well. It is certainly possible that Paul, sharing the prevailing conceptions of his cultural and religious context, did think that Adam had destroyed an earlier divine plan whereby human beings would not have been the divided beings described in Romans 7 (even after the reconciliation with God effected by Christ), even if the death and resurrection of Jesus had never been part of the picture.

But while that is possible, Paul's reflection leads inexorably to conclusions that cannot logically fit in with such an hypothesis. The proof is already evident in the antithetical parallelism between Adam and Christ that Paul draws in Romans 5. For there Sin, which was victorious over Adam, is shown to be definitively defeated, even in its consequences, by Jesus.[213]

One might object that the human being continues to be divided, serving the mechanism of Sin with its 'flesh' or human condition. That is true, and that is precisely what forces Paul's logic to take a further step in Romans 8. Quite obviously, the anthropology structured there, vis-à-vis the eschatological panorama opened up by Jesus' resurrection, is far superior to anything to be expected from the unrestricted continuation of the paradisiacal situation of Adam and his descendants. Faced with the perspective of 'the glorious freedom of the children of God', we cannot conceive this gift as a *means* of repairing a divine plan supposedly undone by Adam's sin.[214]

In short, Paul's logic manages to give a full, mature meaning to the human condition *as it is*, i.e., to the condition that all human beings know, however subject it may be to the Law, Sin, and Death. And this will be highly meaningful when the perspectives of evolution show humanity to what extent, and with what mechanisms, it can and should take charge of an incomplete creation.[215]

That is why I said it matters little whether Paul was thinking explicitly of a plan which, from the very beginning of creation and independent of Adam's will, would place the universe in humanity's hands. First, because Paul's logic leads to that idea anyway. Second, because even if Paul never thought at all about such an idea for want of perspectives about an evolving creation, we today might possess the transcendent data, in a continuing line with his, that would lead us in that direction even without Paul.

Remember that Paul felt it essential to displace the attention and infantile fear of the human being focused on its own salvation, the latter being conceived as the successful passing of a test whose stipulations had been fixed in the Law by God. Hence Paul opposed Faith to any and all calculations based on the fulfillment of that Law (i.e., works). It was that Faith that would characterize the mature, adult human being.

But it was not easy to move away from the conception that human existence on earth is a trial or test, devoid of meaning in itself. The problem was that one had to move beyond the conception of freedom as a *danger*. And so Paul, as we saw, ignored the option of our 'inner humanity', simply assuming that it was *good*.

In doing that, Paul did not leave human freedom in suspense, with its free will facing good and evil. Instead he gave that freedom its full meaning: i.e., the possibility of carrying out its own projects in reality. Evil was not the object of this freedom; rather, it ambushed the human being when it was in the process of carrying out its plans. God, in other words, had placed within human beings a creative impulse like his own, one that was destined to create love, like his own. Human free will was not exercised in accepting or rejecting that impulse; it came into play *further on*. It was not involved in a direct option between good or evil. It was operative in the deployment of energies that brought goodness and love to fulfillment in an alien world.

Thus human projects were basically threatened by the mechanism of all the various laws—natural, cultural, and moral. Due to the *easiness* with which they become tried and well-beaten tracks for energy, they detour the initial project from its goal. In the face of this easiness, free will made its choice: not between what is good or evil *in itself*, but between the good of being free and a person and the evil of not being that but a mere thing. *Evil* for the human being was letting oneself be carried along as a thing by any type of law. In other words: the radical loss of meaning for a human being's activity, its Death.[216]

Once Paul completely eliminated the possibility of identifying Good and Evil as real, direct objects of human action, the criterion of the latter became creativity itself: i.e., the best energy calculus and arrangement in a circuit that was possible for love in an ever-changing and problematic context.

All this begins to surface in Paul. And it converges with data that have surfaced in the realm of the sciences that study the mechanisms of evolution. The latter data are tending to become the overall frame, beyond the limits of any verifiable experience,[217] for the meaning and orientation of human action and the human being itself.

Our familiar world would seem to be heading down the road of entropy toward coldness, after an initial explosion (?) of highly concentrated energy. In other words, it seems to be moving toward increasingly undifferentiated and degenerated forms of energy, hence increasingly unusable forms when viewed from the standpoint of the strange spectator and participant known as *homo*.

But here scientists record something that they cannot explain, or do not want to explain, since chance as an explanation is contradictory on its own terms. Within this degeneration of energy there appears and grows a line of *negentropy*. Beings arise who increasingly withdraw their existences from blind chance, who are endowed with a growing adaptation and teleonomy.

How are we to characterize this unexpected but constant direction of energy activity? Not surprisingly, we have seen that in its higher realizations (however you take the word 'higher') this increasingly rich and complex ordering of individual and social circuits corresponds to *love*: a synthesis of centers, or circuit of circuits.

It is here that we would go completely wrong if we were to imagine that evolution *chooses between entropy and negentropy*, just as human freedom supposedly chooses between good and evil.[218]

And this is not so much because 'choosing' is an anthropomorphism. With that I am simply trying to indicate what teleonomy makes clear to the eyes of the most exact scientists. The whole biological universe is not a product of chance, since the latter by itself can have only fortuitous results. It must logically be attributed to some intrinsic quality that is coextensive with the whole universe, *within which* stochastic processes subject to chance would have their place and function. This is obviously the case with the so-called 'higher' beings. It would be a transcendent datum, but a reasonable one, to assume that this structure is proper to all that exists in the domain of our experience, though in primordial forms. Or, if you prefer, that this is the structure of our mind, which organizes that experience.

The mistake of assuming that evolution *chooses between* entropy and negentropy is in the same line as that which makes us think that the human being, through personal will or religion, can cease to be the divided being that it is. Evolution does not choose between alternatives when it confronts entropy and negentropy; it necessarily combines both thermodynamic tendencies. In a context of constant and scarce energy, every performance or realization pre-supposes the simultaneous and complementary use of costly energy and cheap energy. Or, if you prefer the circuit metaphor: a circuit of circuits in which it is always necessary to use differently calibrated fuses to prevent what are consid-ered pathogenic variations in some of the different circuits.

Making choices (out of love) entails a greater or lesser opening up to risk. The 'monstrous' effects in individuals or policies have no other origin, much less a supernatural one. That is the harsh 'law of the members', which will always put some distance between the direction in which projects are aiming and the point they actually reach.

Of course it is not even *verifiable* that something as seemingly simple and common as human freedom exists.[219] But if it does exist and have meaning, it can only have positive meaning within an incomplete creation, where negen-tropy is surely the value but where realization will always entail the use of cheap energy. And all that is framed in an energy calculus where our good faith as well as our prudence comes into play.

(2). In the conclusions we drew from our analysis of Paul in Volume III, we found reasons for 'optimism' and 'pessimism'. Optimism seemed to be implied in the conception of our 'inner humanity' being always oriented by the Spirit toward love and goodness. This contrasted with a correlative pessimism about the possibility of inscribing in reality the projects of that seemingly well-intentioned inner humanity.

One cannot read through the first eight chapters of Romans without noticing the fluctuations in Paul's descriptions of the human 'now' that follows the newness of Jesus. These fluctuations, unique among the New Testament writers, are so many indications, if not of uncertainty, at least of greater fidelity to the complexity of the real world.

On the one hand, *everything* is new. If Jesus has any meaning and signifi-cance, it is that there is nothing to fear (obviously from the enemies: the Law, Sin, and Death). Creation may be incomplete. But if the Creator gave us his own son, as sign and cause of reconciliation, salvation, and filial adoption, and that at the very moment when there was no worth in us to aspire to such a thing, then the reasonable causes for fearing the future have disappeared. We will never be in a worse situation than the one in which everything underwent the most radical change possible.

But all that runs counter to our concrete experience. There we would be inclined to say that *nothing* has changed, at least in some respects. Romans 6, with all its indecision, is noteworthy in this respect. Paul moves from stating a *fact* to urging that fact on us as a *duty*. Which of these two expressions is in line with reality: "Sin will no longer reign over you"; or, "Don't let Sin reign over you any longer"? After reading Romans 5, with its parallel between Adam and

Christ and the announcement of the latter's complete victory, we would say that the *first* version is the right one. And even right now Paul undoubtedly sees something new and great for humanity becoming visible in the following of Jesus.

But doesn't concrete experience as a whole point to the *second* version as the correct one? The great merit of Paul is that he did not sacrifice reality to theory. He took into account the depths of his own experience and treated them with all seriousness. The 'I' that analyzes the failure of the divided human being to realize its projects, after the victory claimed in the previous chapter, has puzzled and surprised Paul's commentators. But that 'I' guarantees Paul's seriousness in trying to keep his transcendent data as close as possible to the empirical reality of human existence. And there, isn't it Death that has the last word? If so, then so does Sin: i.e., the Law, the lack of freedom in Paul's sense of the word, the negation of meaning.

Only the *eschatological* perspective of Romans 8, arising out of the interpretation of Jesus' resurrection, permits Paul to offer an overall response. Twice the words alluding to that perspective (*apocalypse* and *glory*) are linked up with ones alluding to history (creative *adoption* and *freedom*), as if to tell us we should not expect to see what is still an object of hope. It is an object of the hope that is incorporated into our activity as a fundamental, transcendent datum of that activity.

An incomplete creation is what gives human freedom its fullest meaning. But that would be of little use to human beings acting in the future, if the contributions of human freedom to the universe in formation were *cumulative*. On the other hand, they would not mean much either if they were not somehow cumulative. It is precisely the eschatological perspective that maintains the necessary dialectic between those two exigencies of meaning in Paul's thought. That is its one and only function.

Our present-day knowledge of some of the general mechanisms of evolution permits us to give to this transcendent datum, or body of data, content materials that are much closer to the concrete. In our familiar universe, you see, entropy reigns. Even more significantly, the very growth of negentropy does not threaten, much less do away with that reign. The impossibility of any accumulation of the positive is analogically present on different levels.

It shows up first as the inexorable second law of thermodynamics. Although energy is constant, available and usable energy is not. The latter becomes scarcer with every activation of energy, however skillful and rich may be some energy syntheses that manage to appear here and there. That accounts for their numerical minority, or their statistical defeat if you will, which cannot be doubted. Furthermore, with every activation of these syntheses, some usable energy is lost; it degenerates into simpler, more undifferentiated energy.

On the biological level that is what is meant by death, the paradoxical condition of all living beings. The energy cost of each organism, even the simplest, is so high that it translates into an unstable and increasingly costly equilibrium. Finally, the energy is given back to chance (limited by genetics), so that chance can offer the same original possibilities to new organisms. Thus energy that is alive—i.e., that adapts and reproduces—always ends in death, so that the cycle may continue and advance.

What is more, life is characterized by the fact it escapes death, if not individually then at least as a species. Thanks to their genetic components, living beings do not flow into *universal* chance again at the end of their lives. At death the species returns them to a more restricted stochastic process: chance *within* the species. In other words, life reproduces itself by very definition. Yet here, too, entropy plays its role. The qualities acquired by the 'mind' of an individual during the course of its life are not transmitted to the genetic code. Genius or goodness does not pass from parent to child by the easy road of 'inheritance'.

Thus entropy shows up as well on the level of the species: in the unexpected barrier placed between mental mechanisms of adaptation on the one hand and the genetic code on the other. This 'no' to the evolutionist expectations of a Lamarck seemed scandalous at first; but now we see it as a saving thing, even though it may continue to be distressing. Given the energy structure of the universe, that apparently easy and beneficial transmission would lead to an irreparable generalization of entropy. But 'humanity' is not the property of anyone; it does not accumulate in any group, nation, project, or human achievement. And to attempt such an accumulation would be suicidal. It can only be the result of an enterprise that includes all.

Paradoxical as it may seem, then, hope waits for us everywhere. There are no predestined ones because there are no useless ones. In every generation all are confronted with crucial but fleeting dangers and accomplishments. All hold in their hand something precious to save for the future of all the rest. And, luckily, they cannot see it. For if they could, that would make evolution a race, led by the best endowed, toward a universe without problems. What God had left incomplete, as the condition for giving decisive value to human beings, would be completed. If that is not to happen, a price must be paid. The aged and decentered elements of one generation must be handed over again to the limited chance of the next generation. Life must be nurtured with death.

Ideology may be viewed as entropy in thinking. So I need hardly spell out the disastrous ideological results that occur when actual achievements are judged in terms of an unachieved ideal, or of an ideal achieved only in a minute fraction of humanity with great energy means. By ignoring the dialectic of all achievement or realization in this way, the ideal becomes its own negation. In the name of Christianity, for example, a bishop will make such statements as the following about the two dominant sociopolitical systems, capitialism and socialism: "We must have the courage to break with this limitation into two systems. We must cease to be puppets before the cobra that is hypnotizing us with its two big eyes and jump *outside*. Neither capitalism, nor communism, nor the ideology of national security. *Something new is needed.*"[220] So we must wait and hope. But for what exactly? Or how long? And in the meantime?

What is not noticed is the mechanism that explains the inhuman aspect or aspects of both major systems. And that mechanism, analogically of course, is nothing more nor less than the violation, in the name of entropy, of the barrier between somatic modifications and the genetic code. It is the old temptation to make the good easy by turning it into automatism and habit, or to survive by an increasing expenditure of energy that should have been invested in other solutions of a broader and more basic nature.

In that sense it is surely true that the cobra does not have a third eye, however much one may talk about the 'ideology of national security'. When entropy deprives the two big eyes of their hypnotizing power, each develops a supplementary eye to ensure 'order'. Thus 'national security' is nothing more than the ideological name for the repression needed to keep the victims of the energy-waste quiet and at work. And that squandering of energy is provoked by the fear of risk and death, by the lack of faith in the resurrection of the ideal that was once creative and is now only conservative.[221] Ever more 'violent' means are applied to sustain the initial values, nobody noticing that it is this 'sin' that leads most quickly to Death because it turns those values into empty things.

(3). As we have seen, every problematic concerned with meaning bets on a certain 'eschatology': *in the end* we shall see who was right in giving this or that axiological direction to his or her life and activity.

In the circumstances in which the destiny of the human being is carried out, that wager or bet will be justified only if Death is defeated. Value needs reality. Nothing makes sense if nothing lasts. And as we have already noted, not just any type of 'resurrection' will do. Only a resurrection that liberates us from Sin's condemnation to meaninglessness can justify the risk entailed in freedom. And justify it to the point where, whatever the real-life discharge of that freedom may have been, the human being can say 'at the end': it was worthwhile.[222]

We have seen how this perspective, drawn from the experiences of the risen Jesus and set against the backdrop of the experience of the divided human being, gave originality to Paul's thinking in his treatment of eschatology. His anthropology would collapse totally, meaningless, if the resurrection were merely the warmup for an uncertain judgment rather than the result of one already known by faith.

Precisely because the universal resurrection is, for Paul, the outcome of a victory of Grace over Sin, it is also the manifestation of the freedom proper to the children of God the creator. The systematic dominion of Sin over the 'flesh' rendered invisible the work of freedom, 'alienating' its fruits and thereby negating freedom itself. So that the human being, faced with the results, feels compelled to say: 'This is not what I wanted'.

Jesus did not want the Cross and Death—despite what many speculative christologies tell us. He had to pass through them so that the power of his freedom applied to the project of establishing the kingdom would be manifested. And such is the case with every human being. It is thus that human freedom meets up with the *definitive* on the road of meaning. That meeting is 'outside' history, in the sense that, so long as history lasts, the 'Flesh' will always subject that freedom to Sin, hence failure on the plane of meaningfulness. But the meeting is 'inside' history because what is called to be definitive, once tested and examined closely, is what was done by the human being in the face of history and its complexities, and to give meaning and value to the latter.

In the definitive reality, then, the human being who has been an historical agent will recognize, and at the same time have difficulty recognizing (without the usual entropy), his or her 'resurrected' work in history. The same thing that happens with Jesus in his paschal experiences.

Talk of 'resurrection', of course, seems to be so far removed from a serious vision of evolutionary reality that, at first glance, we might be tempted to say that none of the mechanisms of evolution studied by science can have any relationship with it. But let us set aside the positive or negative fascination of supposedly religious terms, such as 'resurrection', and look at some of the data concerning entropy and its principal consequence, Death, in the circuits that carry on the evolutionary process, or have carried it on so far at least.

We have seen that the only world where human freedom can play a crucial role is a world in which there is a constant quantity of energy and the constant danger of its degenerating, a world where the achievements of negentropy do not accumulate.

Every organism has to go back and use the same common energy left by its predecessors. The latter must leave that energy behind rather than corner it for themselves, must lose their energy autonomy. For that to happen, time and age, the visible representatives of entropy, must make the attained ordering of energy increasingly costly until at last it cannot be sustained. This degeneration of energy, which takes energy out of the hands of every organism, human being, group, and society in order to give it back to the chance of their successors, is Death. So the acceptance of Death, as opposed to the miserly, egotistical, and ultimately futile desire to prolong one's own energy autonomy unrestrictedly, becomes a precondition for new and better achievements.

I say 'better' because there is one more datum, which has to do with a certain form of 'resurrection'. Through those successive circuits, in which deactivation and death have had their necessary function and will continue to have it, there has been emerging something that is not verifiable in the short term (of a generation or two) but is verifiable in the overall process: *the growth of negentropy*.

The evolution that began with extremely simple or poor biological circuits has been gradually moving toward incomparably greater richness and complexity. The human species *is* that *already*, but it is also true of its *achievements* over the long term. We saw, for example, that the overcoming of entropy *always* entails information. But we also see that information, following the same process, has become *conscious* in beings endowed with a central nervous system, and *digital* in humanity; thus its possibilities have been growing slowly but surely.

Nothing is more shocking for human 'intentionality' at every level than its own ending and that of its designs: i.e., Death. But with the epistemology suggested to us by the mechanisms of evolution, we find that what seems to be an ending is transformed into a new beginning: invisible and anguishing, to be sure, but not meaningless. Instead of being merely dispossessed of its autonomous energy, our mind comes to understand and appreciate the reason for the dispossession. It is for the benefit—gratuitous and uncontrollable but no less certain—of successors, who are to direct the goals pursued in the life of one person into new channels.

In the meantime we must admit that death changes in meaning when a shift takes place—on the individual level as well as on the sociopolitical level—from a linear logic of cause and effect to a circuit logic. Our own death and that of everyone else is redeemed from uselessness by *the others*: i.e., by freedom invested in love. It is not *directly* our own individual resurrection, mere 'reincarnation', prolonging our autonomy beyond death, that deprives Death, the great enemy of meaningfulness, of its victory. Victory over death is, before anything else, the victory of love over egotism.

This conception is profoundly related to Paul's thinking about the decisiveness of 'Faith' operative in love. Since that Faith takes love seriously, it does not seek any easy escape from the problem of death. Such escapes translate logically into an egotism that is conservative and ultimately death-dealing.

That being clear, we might well ask ourselves here if the reflection just offered above is not too quick to discard certain basic preconditions for a complete victory of meaningfulness over meaninglessness. Is it really a finished and complete solution to all that we know about death in this new context?

In reading what follows, let us remember that *any* response to the above question constitutes a transcendent datum, whether it be affirmative or negative. That does not mean, of course, that everything is equally "reasonable" and worthwhile in this realm of the empirically unverifiable. Although transcendent data are largely 'self-validating', they are to some extent subject to a criterion of coherence or consistency with what experience teaches us on a more modest plane.

We have seen that meaning already triumphs over death *somehow* in the negative transcendent datum offered by Gregory Bateson: i.e., that the species redeems the death of the individual. And this despite the fact that he is talking about a death without resurrection, and that the cessation of autonomous life seems to be the supreme example of meaninglessness.

But let us look at that more closely. We know that entropy has to be incorporated into those circuits that guide the process toward the growth of *negentropy*: i.e., order and meaning. But entropy proceeds with its work. The richer and completer the syntheses betokening the apparent triumph of negentropy, the more energy 'spent' on them. The 'spent' energy does not disappear; it is degraded into increasingly less usable forms.

So we have a desperate race against the clock. Concentrated forms of energy, such as oil, which has been in formation and reserve for millions of years, are 'burned up' (i.e., deactivated) in a few generations. In the best of cases, the energy entailed in maintaining the life of a growing humanity on this planet will find cheap access to new forms of 'practically' inexhaustible energies: e.g., solar energy or the energy buried in every atom.

But our word 'practically' is a cover for a false illusion of eternity. To those who are on the verge of energy collapse, the facile use of solar energy for the same purposes may bring a sigh of relief. But the sun is cooling down, and only certain types of atoms can be used to liberate the energies of others. So the calculations, however stretched out, move steadily and inexorably toward zero. We can disregard that, as if a very long period of time were equivalent to eternity. But the edifice being built by negentropy on the existing energy base will crumble one day, for want of a base. At least that is what we know at the moment.

Now if death is to be justified as meaningful by the definitive value of the edifice constructed, as a sacrifice for that, will it be justified when the ultimate sources of energy available to humanity are already being visibly exhausted?

The above reflection, you see, seems to have value insofar as negentropy can promise the *definitive*. When we act *as if* its future were truly unlimited. But if that in fact is not the case, it really matters little to meaning whether the endpoint is relatively near or far. The edifice to which the human being consecrated its life and offered up its death will prove to be nothing more than a mysterious wave that crested and fell and grew calm in an immobile sea.

Paul proposes something different as the final perspective: the world of negentropy freed from entropy forever because withdrawn definitively from time. What was built in time will go on existing as a manifestation of definitive meaningfulness. The significance of Jesus of Nazareth for every human being will appear only when Death is defeated, only when negentropy (i.e., growing consciousness) can peek over the barrier now placed in its way by time (subjected to entropy) and be conscious not only of the fragile, present moment but of the total and definitive meaning constructed in history.

Now there is an important objection that can be raised against this perspective. Since it abolishes time, that eschatological manifestation has to be some sort of new creative act. Hence it has to come from a power superior to that of the elements to which concrete experience introduces us.

I would only ask my readers to consider something that may surprise them. Consider some of the words used with such abandon by scientists, including Gregory Bateson: *negentropy*, for example, with its train of teleonomy and meaning. These apparently innocent words already in fact appeal to a power superior to all the elements offered us by experience. Negentropy is as surprising and 'supernatural' as resurrection in a world where energy is degraded. And all the attempts to give chance as the ultimate explanation are nothing more than an infantile logical fallacy.[223]

We have here two opposed transcendent data, and we must make a real choice between them rather than avoiding it or faking it. All I am claiming here is that one of them seems to me to be more reasonable, because it is also the one more logically consistent with the data that concrete experience offers us within its verifiable limits.

II

When I began my study of Jesus of Nazareth in Volume II, I asked why and to what extent the repetition of a past christological creation today, however biblical it might be, would better facilitate the meaningfulness of Jesus than a christological creation arising out of our own partial, anguished context here and now. To exemplify the point, I offered a poetic expression of the good news of Jesus that had been written by someone intimately associated with the realities of our continent.[224]

As we saw, the language of Leonardo Boff's text was noticeably more comprehensible to any human being, religious or not, who is seeking meaning for his or her existence. It isn't that Boff did not mention Jesus by name. It is that he did not interpret his significance in categories that would artificially limit its scope for all those who had not studied the metaphysical proofs for the existence of God, or who did not think in the categories reserved to small groups already united by a particular creed.

As I bring my work to a close here, I would like to bring together some of what I have said in these pages by citing a brief excerpt from another poetic text that originated in our Latin American context. It comes from someone who is not a Christian, who may be assumed to be an atheist. That will not seem so strange if readers have taken note of the contents of these volumes:

There are dead bodies in the twilight and dead bodies in the heat of midday. Dead bodies that set and dead bodies that rise like the sun. Adolescents who put in their last smile all their faith in life and more than life. Girls that gave birth to their sacrifice, and gave it a name, and nursed it at the breast. And when the machine gun rattled, they covered it with their pretty body so that it might be saved. And the sacrifice was saved. Just barely, but saved. For that reason, because in a grey, obscure place, where no one was capable of giving a gift of ten minutes or ten pesos, these men and women, sober and immortal, were capable of giving their lives, for that reason their defeat is joined and knitted with the earth. And buds and is born again with banners and dreams that flame into promises happily fulfilled . . .[225]

Some will ask: And what does *Jesus* add? An initial response might be: Why would he have to add anything? Couldn't this be a way—conscious or unconscious, dependent or independent—of saying the same thing? May we not have here a parable in which, under other faces, characters, and idioms, we again encounter the meaning of what happened in the life of Jesus of Nazareth himself, a meaning transmitted by invisible pathways?

If there is *something more*, and undoubtedly there is, it is not anything that Jesus would add by himself from the pages of the gospel message. It is what contact and involvement with the problems, crises, and conflicts of history, shouldered in the light of the first interpretation, have gradually been contributing to the meaning and significance of his good news.

If Volume V has achieved its modest objective, perhaps there will be deeper answers for the questions that the poem itself leaves unanswered: What is more worth the trouble to 'protect'? What 'children' and from what evils? How are we to measure the sacrifices destined to 'survive' without any egotism or illusions? Where and how is the sacrifice saved, 'just barely, but saved'?

Perhaps my readers may find in the reflections up to this point elements of an answer that they would have sought in vain in the letter of the gospel message. Perhaps it is not illusory to think, contrary to the assumption of those who would like to have been contemporaries of Jesus or members of the early Church, that we today can give more complete answers to such questions, in accordance with the 'spirit of Jesus'.

Notes

Introduction: A Jesus for Today

1. José Ramón Guerrero, *El otro Jesús,* p. 15. And he adds the obvious reason that is familiar to readers of these volumes: "If the early Christian community had not one but four gospels of Jesus of Nazareth, thereby adapting his message to specific, concrete situations and cultures, the believing community today must discover and formulate *its own* gospel. 'There is only *one* Christ, of course, but many christologies. No one possesses the one Christ, but everybody has a christology' (H. Zahrnt, *Dios no puede morir,* Bilbao, 1971, p. 197)."

2. In Volume II, Appendix I, I noted how John or the author of the fourth Gospel carefully distinguished at times between the 'contemporary' understanding of an event and the 'later' understanding based especially on the paschal experiences.

3. With all the resultant inconsistencies that cannot be salvaged. The Synoptics tell us that only at the end of his Galilean ministry did Jesus reveal that he was the Messiah to Peter, and perhaps the rest of his disciples. John's Gospel tells us that this revelation took place much earlier. The most varied messianic titles are applied to Jesus from the very first chapter of John's Gospel on, from the time he was baptized by John the Baptist if not earlier.

4. We find positive evidence of this awareness, even before the appearance of the *Diatessaron,* in the rejection and ultimate condemnation of Marcion's view. Marcion noticed the different theologies in the Gospels, even in the Synoptics, and concluded that it was necessary to *unify* the gospel material theologically. In condemning Marcion, the Church was not denying the theological differences of the various Gospels; it was choosing to safeguard their plurality as a difficult but indispensable feature of historical fidelity.

5. Which is something very different from showing how he comes to be identified positively with the Son of God in and through his concrete history.

6. Thus important features of Jesus' preaching can be ignored. A book entitled *The Imitation of Christ,* no less, can say: "Every time I have been out among human beings, I came back less human"!

7. "The disappearance of the humanity of Jesus Christ behind his divinity affected all of Christian piety, particularly its teaching on the sacraments. Just as the proximity of Jesus as human being was erased, so the Eucharist was made unapproachable and remote. More and more conditions for receiving it were imposed. The host was elevated repeatedly for veneration. Various forms of pious adoration were created. The place of its exposition and the ciborium took on more importance and dignity than the eucharistic meal. The logical consequence of estrangement from the humanity of Jesus Christ was a series of secondary mediations that grew out of all proper importance: relics as incalculable treasures to be used as commodities or plundered; unchecked veneration of

the saints; and the transfer to Mary of various expressions and titles that belonged to Jesus Christ as the new Adam and the prototype of redeemed humanity" (Guerrero, p. 41).

8. In this brief presentation I am not exaggerating Bultmann's pejorative estimation of the results obtained in the quest for the historical Jesus. I am oversimplifying the matter, however, insofar as I do not consider the historical backdrop that helps to explain the direction Bultmann's exegesis took. He was influenced by the criticism of earlier 'liberal' exegesis, which tended to keep reducing the significance of Jesus as the certain historical data about him grew less. Bultmann attempted, with some success, to stifle that tendency by rejecting any thought of a 'history of Jesus', without rejecting Jesus' significance for human beings. He proposed a different exegetical approach for christology: the existential interpretation of the Jesus of faith, the Jesus of the New Testament 'christologies'. Bultmann's 'demythologization' must be understood in that context.

9. J. R. Guerrero, p. 74. His citation comes from W. Trilling, *Jesús y los problemas de su historicidad,* Barcelona, 1970. Guerrero then notes the 'surprising contradictions' in the life of Jesus and cites E. Trocmé: "This mystery already is a harbinger of the uncertainties faced by the evangelists and theologians of the first century. Neither the historians nor the theologians have been able to eliminate it completely, nor will they ever be able to do so. No biographer will be able to do anything but spell out the data of the mystery. Then each one will have to try for an intuitive grab at Jesus" (E. Trocmé, *Jesús de Nazaret visto por los testigos de su vida,* Spanish edition, Barcelona, 1974, pp. 170–171; English edition, *Jesus As Seen by His Contemporaries,* Philadelphia: Westminster Press, 1973).

10. This *lack of concretion* in the case of the historical Jesus is practically turned into a basic principle by Guerrero. In terms reminiscent of a christology from above, he writes: "Every political project is associated with a limited space of time. Jesus takes into account the total temporal order, aiming at a radical transformation of everyone and everything and the attainment of a new society" (*El otro Jesús,* p. 105). His principle would annul not only a political project, but any type of project at all; because any performance in history is rooted in a particular, limited time. Besides, it is nothing but a flagrant contradiction to assert that Jesus the human being takes into account *the total temporal order.*

11. See the Trocmé quote in note 9. I have followed Guerrero's exposition, only by way of example, because his starting point seemed closer to my own. But readers may recall my remarks about Hans Küng's position in Volume II, Chapter 6, section II. It is just as problematic to base *faith* on an historical (?) Jesus who transcends all conflicts.

12. It is worth noting that the fundamental criterion of the 'orthodoxy' of any Christian interpretation collapses, if there is no faithfulness to the history of the person. After the Trocmé citation given in note 9, Guerrero goes on to say that "the mystery of Jesus lies in the fact that he was and ever remains the object contemplated by all but never possessed by anyone, *not even by his disciples*" (Guerrero, *El otro Jesús,* p. 74). Now if 'possessing' Jesus means 'monopolizing and controlling him', or making one interpretation of him that is valid once and for all, then I would agree with Guerrero. But the Trocmé citation talks about each person making an 'intuitive grab at Jesus'. It is hard to imagine how we are to choose orthodoxy among 'intuitive grabs'.

13. Let me pursue this problem with the example I have been using. Guerrero denounces the 'ideologizing' of christology (*El otro Jesús,* pp. 55f.), and particularly the "ideological process of interiorizing and spiritualizing the content of the Christian

faith" (ibid., p. 57). But then he proceeds to write the following: "In the beatitudes Jesus shows us how the values of the kingdom transform the human heart. The kingdom affects the inner bearing of people, not their outer bearing. The beatitudes present three pairs of terms: *the poor—the rich, the hungry—the sated, the sad—the happy.* The first group in each pair is opposed to the second because they have been interiorizing the values of the kingdom and hence will possess it. A certain attitude *now* means full possession of the kingdom *later*" (ibid., p. 135).

My readers can easily guess which terms I would have italicized. I just don't see how Guerrero (ibid., p. 105) can accept the terrible ideologization contained in the words of another author he cites: "The notions of success and failure, of victory and defeat, are displaced. The originality of Jesus did not lie in moving away from the revolutionary strategy but in turning upside down the terms that define any and every strategy. The here-and-now triumph of the oppressor is already his defeat, and the defeat of the oppressed is already their triumph, as the beatitudes suggest (G. Crespy, *El mito de Jesús*)."

14. The most serious grounding for this hermeneutic approach up to now, as far as I know, is the work of Hans-Georg Gadamer, *Wahrheit und Methode,* pp. 250–255 (English translation entitled *Truth and Method*). This reference is most important because I think his approach, in different terminology, largely dovetails with my own rehabilitation of anthropological faith in Volume I of this series (see Gadamer, *Wahrheit und Methode,* pp. 261–269); and that methodological approach governs my present hermeneutic vis-à-vis Jesus of Nazareth.

15. Karl Rahner rightly points out the following: "If then the ordinary theology current today is to be asked why what it has told *us* is insufficiently clear, by 'us' is meant we as we must be today; for man's unique standpoint in history is inescapably given him in advance and helps to determine the perspective within which we have to consider God's eternal truths too, if we are really going to let them become a reality of mind, heart and life in our personal existence. This is not to say that it is in general particularly profitable for theology to take as the explicit starting-point of a critical consideration of the average christology current today, any characteristic features of just that spiritual situation which has been imposed upon us, insofar as they are apprehended *reflexively.* Such a method is seldom successful. . . . It is preferable simply to look at the facts, that is to say at christology itself—always providing that one has the courage to ask questions, to be dissatisfied, to think with the mind and heart one actually has, and not with the mind and heart one is supposed to have" (Rahner, "Current Problems in Christology," *Theological Investigations I,* p. 153).

16. Guerrero, *El otro Jesús,* p. 315. Reading Guerrero and the other quotes from his work given earlier, we find it difficult to decide for sure whether his words here are aiming at the same target that I am. Sometimes he seems to be, but at other times he does not seem to be at all.

17. Of course there are still enormous gaps in our knowledge of both universal and biological evolution. See, in particular, the section written by Paul Overhage in the joint work by him and Karl Rahner: Rahner and Overhage, *El problema de la hominización.* Although we cannot expect to know everything, however, certain general lines seem to promise new discoveries, along with the mental structures that pave the way for them. I shall explore this in greater detail in the following chapter.

18. And there seems to be no hope of changing that situation. If free elections are limited to those who enjoy a privileged position in the global system, how can we expect them to deliberately opt for policies that will drastically reduce their own privileges?

That would seem to explain the hopelessness, with its mixture of cynicism and good intentions, that marks 'liberal' North Americans when they confront the criticisms or demands of the Third World.

19. Without any dialectical process involving the negation of the negation. Betting on the ultimate victory of socialist powers or superpowers, these people put off or sacrifice the steps that could be taken toward a socialism of their own.

20. As we saw in Volume I, Bateson suggests that religion—I would prefer to say *religious faith*—can invest political intentionality with the broad ecological dimension it needs, as opposed to any individualistic or partisan focus. Machoveč seems to be saying something similar when he insists we need religious or spiritual traditions, specifically that of Jesus, to resolve crucial problems that even successful socialism leaves unanswered. Moreover, those who imagine *a priori* that the Christian message is valid only for the individual or the interior life are directly in opposition to the teaching of Vatican II (see GS, 11).

21. I need hardly point out that these points are also valid for the christology discussed in Volume IV. But that sort of christology does not need them quite so desperately, for reasons that will be made obvious as we proceed.

22. The postpaschal data on the messianism of Jesus already retrace his significance back to the problems posed by the long history of Israel. He is the solution to those traditional problems, which ultimately lead back to reflection on the origin of the world. Particularly worth noting in this connection is the theological thrust of Luke's genealogy of Jesus: Luke 3:23–38.

23. This tendency will grow stronger and find even more explicit symbolic expression after Paul. See Col 1:15–17; Eph 1:10; Rev 1:8.17; Rev 21:6; etc.

24. Remember that by 'mix' here I mean the use of an element taken in isolation from its context and simply 'added' to another element. Elements coming from different christologies do not constitute a mix when they are joined, each in accordance with its own proper context, to *multiply* our information.

25. For his original statement see Julian Huxley, *Evolution in Action,* p. 141.

Chapter I: Toward a New Context

26. P. Teilhard de Chardin, *L'activation de l'énergie,* p. 80. See also Rideau, *The Thought of Teilhard de Chardin,* p. 302.

27. Paradoxically, this 'quantum' leap has been described for some time in philosophical terms as a *'qualitative* leap'. Teilhard writes: "In every domain, when anything exceeds a certain measurement, it suddenly changes its aspect, condition, or nature" (Teilhard de Chardin, *The Phenomenon of Man,* p. 78). To explain the paradox, we can make use of Bateson's differentiation between 'quantity' (quantitative element) and 'number' (qualitative element). The former might also be considered continuous 'quantity', the latter 'mold' or 'pattern'. The latter is a quantum element, being made up of discontinuous quantities, and hence is equivalent to what philosophy calls a 'qualitative difference.' See Gregory Bateson, *Mind and Nature,* pp. 49–53.

28. On the notion of 'threshold' see what Teilhard de Chardin has to say about the phyletic *shift* embodied in hominization (*The Phenomenon of Man,* p. 174). In a letter of November 20, 1918, Teilhard formulates an important principle for understanding 'thresholds' while avoiding false brands of mysticism or esotericism: "*The mystery of every circle of the world* lies *in the next circle*: that's the principle that should protect the mystic from every fanciful dream and every absurdity" (Rideau, *The Thought of Teilhard de Chardin,* p. 434, note 17).

29. At the moment I am writing these pages, people are debating whether the manufacture of neutron bombs will increase or decrease the possibility of total nuclear war between the superpowers. Israel justifies its destruction of an atomic reactor in Iraq as a 'defensive' act. Disarmament by the superpowers is an urgent issue. There is worry about the growth of nuclear power in smaller countries; their local atomic wars might trigger a general conflict. And so it goes.

30. In Marx's interpretation, the dialectic of Hegel would be characteristic of the hold (in Teilhard's image); though dynamic, Hegel's dialectic would be nothing but an *explanation* of the world. Though he never framed himself within strictly evolutionary coordinates (only vaguely sensed in his own day, despite Darwin), Marx would occupy a place similar to that of Paul or Jesus insofar as his project of a classless society implies a quest going beyond the boundaries of a hold that is presumably static in terms of axiology. The possession of a type of thought that is better suited to evolutionary categories, if it does not actually require them, is not peculiar to religion alone in the past. Readers will appreciate the fact that I am using the term 'evolution' here in the broad sense. In the strictest and most precise sense, it would obviously be opposed to the common idea of creation (as conceived in the Bible or other cosmogonic myths) and, in the political realm, to the idea of revolution or any qualitative leap.

31. It will always be a frustrating and sterile exercise to ask history: What would have happened if . . .? The innumerable quantity of variables in it means that we can only consider *grosso modo* the influences we really can verify as being at work.

32. See Harvey Cox, *The Secular City,* especially the first chapter on the biblical roots of secularization.

33. If Hegel tries to do that, his idealism in conceiving the evolutionary process of the Absolute Spirit prevents him from mooring his dialectic to poles that represent real groups or interests. That is the reason for Marx's negative critique, not only of Hegel, but also of all 'idealism'.

34. And even for christologies 'from below' insofar as they begin with the historical Jesus but fail to perceive any intrinsic relationship between that individual history and the larger forces which, without negating human freedom or using it cunningly as their instrument (Hegel), direct the great lines of history. That is why christologies 'from below' become atemporal and ahistorical as soon as they think they have determined the significance of the 'historical Jesus'.

35. As will be seen in what follows, I am not talking about *metaphysical* analogy which starts from the more universal idea of *being* and enables human beings to conceive of beings which, by their essence, are beyond all empirical perception. This may be the reason why some authors, Bateson for example, prefer to use the term 'homology' instead of 'analogy'. That term *formally* brings together data deriving from all levels of the biological process.

36. Gregory Bateson, *Steps to an Ecology of Mind,* p. 154.

37. This may in large part explain the discrediting of Teilhard de Chardin by a significant segment of the scientific community when his works began to be published and to arouse enthusiasm (1955 on). To some extent this negative reaction was due to logical positivism, which has now been partially superceded. But it may also have been due to the fact that Teilhard was a pioneer in this field, and that *loose* thinking dominated his approach too much even though he was a recognized scientist. Bateson had the advantage over him in that he exercised *strict* thinking in even *stricter* scientific disciplines, if you will permit me to put it that way: e.g., cybernetics.

38. Bateson, *Steps,* p. 74.

39. Actually this does not even constitute a 'mental' operation or 'information', since

the minimum unit of the latter is a 'difference that makes a difference' (see Bateson, *Mind and Nature,* p. 99). Knowing the numbers that have come up on a roulette wheel constitutes a difference, but the meaninglessness of the sequence results in the fact that it makes no difference to me. If all I get from this difference is a series of unrelated numbers, then there is no difference between the before and after of my 'reception' of those numbers in a photographic way.

40. See Bateson, *Mind and Nature,* pp. 3 f., 109 f.

41. Note my comments on Monod's peculiar use of the word 'chance' further on in this chapter, pp. 35 f.

42. See Bateson, *Mind and Nature,* p. 110.

43. Ibid., p. 30.

44. Ibid., pp. 121f.

45. Ibid., p. 123.

46. See ibid. (pp. 48, 112, etc.) for the difference between causality integrating 'mental' processes and the causality operative between billiard balls.

47. See Jacques Monod, *Chance and Necessity,* pp. 8 f.

48. This is inferred from the fact that the genetic instructions are not mere repetitions. The responses vary according to the needs of the organism. In case of a cut or mutilation, certain members or parts of them are reproduced, not the entire organism. This is a sign that the 'good' of the organism is present, coded somehow, in the information processed by the genetic 'mind'.

49. See Chapter 2, Section I in this volume.

50. The reply that Monod would give to this question, probably without admitting that his own working hypotheses suffer from the same thing, is that analogy is a sort of 'animism'. He defines the latter as follows: "Animist belief, as I am visualizing it here, consists essentially in a projection into inanimate nature of man's awareness of the *intensely teleonomic* functioning of his own central nervous system" (*Chance and Necessity,* p. 30). The italics are mine, to indicate that Monod himself sees purpose or teleonomy growing in 'intensity' with evolution.

51. Monod, *Chance and Necessity,* p. 3.

52. Ibid., p. 9 and *passim.* In Chapter 2 we shall consider another attempt by Monod to evade teleology.

53. Monod, *Chance and Necessity,* pp. 112–113.

54. On the historical development of science since the Renaissance and its relationship with final causality see the judicious comments in Part Two of W. T. Stace, *Religion and the Modern Mind.* Undoubtedly one of the main reasons for the aversion of present-day science to final causality is the direct use of 'finalism' or 'purpose' in nature, by religion, to prove the existence of God. Perhaps that is why Monod equates 'analogy' with primitive sorts of religious 'animism'.

55. Bateson, *Mind and Nature,* pp. 127–130.

56. On this whole matter of 'formal' analogy based on 'mental' relations, see the discussion as to whether cybernetic machines can 'think' in Douglas R. Hofstadter, "Meta-magical Themes," *Scientific American,* May 1981. He presents an interesting debate among three advanced students in different fields: the physiochemical sciences, biology, and philosophy.

57. P. Teilhard de Chardin, *The Phenomenon of Man,* p. 71.

58. One 'christological' mistake of Freud in *Civilization and Its Discontents* was to examine the 'pinpoint' fact of Jesus' message about love of neighbor in association with the instinctual base of society as a whole. In any such comparison the Christian

commandment must come out looking utopian and socially insane. Much of the ambiguity in Freud's own thinking about this precept derives from this inadequate comparison. Taken as a 'pinpoint' commandment, love of neighbor is either a rule for minorities rather than societies, or a utopian folly if intended for the latter. But Freud's mistake here points us toward the proper comparison: i.e., the gradual formation of the precept of *agapé* out of the forces of *eros*. Marcuse picks up Freud's effort and spells out the process in *Eros and Civilization*.

59. Bateson, *Steps*, p. 74.

60. Bateson, *Steps*, pp. 75 f., 153 f.

61. Cited in J. L. Segundo, *Faith and Ideologies*, pp. 259–260.

62. Ibid., p. 259.

63. The most important corrective for human thinking is love: Bateson, *Steps*, pp. 446–447.

64. And since things are associated with human lives, it is easy for this attitude toward things and their use to wreak havoc on human beings as well, especially on foreigners, immigrants, distant peoples and cultures, etc.

65. In the play *Zoo,* based on Vercors *Les animaux dénaturés,* the author presents us with the find of an animal half way between other primates and *homo sapiens*. He thus poses questions we are all too ready to conceal under the basic contrast between animal and human being. Would such a being have *rights*? If it were put to work for human beings, should it be paid? Can it be used as a *mere instrument* like domestic livestock, and even slaughtered and eaten? The author suggests that we human beings have turned ourselves into a kind of 'club', fixed arbitrary standards of admission, and accorded rights only to those who qualify for membership. Other animals and things are used as mere instruments.

Chapter II: Jesus from the Standpoint of the Primordial

66. The main points of doubt or ignorance remaining about these evolutionary mechanisms can be found in *El problema de la hominización* by Karl Rahner and Paul Overhage. But it seems to me that, in the more scientific part, Overhage equates the points that still remain obscure, which are numerous and important, with a supposed weakness of the evolutionist theory in general.

67. Monod, *Chance and Necessity,* pp. 31–32. And he adds: "For my part I am most of all struck by the intellectual spinelessness of this philosophy" (p. 32).

68. Writing about the difference between artificial and natural objects, Monod discusses a man-made knife as an example of the former: "The object renders in material form the pre-existent intention that gave birth to it, and its form is accounted for by the performance expected of it even before it takes shape. It is another story altogether with the river or the rock which we know, or believe, to have been molded by the free play of physical forces to which we cannot attribute any design, any 'project' or purpose. Not, that is, if we accept the basic premise of the scientific method, to wit, that nature is *objective* and not *projective*" (ibid., p. 3).

But to what is he referring with the term 'nature', which he contrasts with the artificial? A little later on he writes: "The last of these examples is a classic one of functional adaptation in living beings, and I have cited it only to emphasize how arbitrary and pointless it would be to deny that the *natural* [Segundo italics] organ, the eye, represents the materialization of a 'purpose'—that of picking up images—while this is indisputably also the origin of the camera. . . . Every artifact is a product made by a living being which through it expresses, in a particularly conspicuous manner, one of the fundamental characteristics common to all living beings without exception: that of being *objects endowed with a purpose or project,* which at the same time they exhibit in their structure and carry out through their performances (such as, for instance, the making of artifacts). Rather than reject this idea (as certain biologists have tried to do), it is indispensable to recognize that it is essential to the very definition of living beings. We shall maintain that the latter are distinct from all other structures or systems present in the universe through this characteristic property, which we shall call *teleonomy*" (ibid., p. 20).

69. Moreover, the immense variety of possibilities open to chance favors a certain general stability, since the chance variants are counteracted by others. The assumption is that this 'conservative' tendency of chance, hence of genetics in general, would prevail if 'natural selection' *from outside* did not convert it into an *oriented* process. See Bateson, *Mind and Nature,* pp. 179 f., and Monod, *Chance and Necessity,* p. 110.

70. Francisco Hunneus, "Una función cientifico-cultural del concepto de Gestalt," pp. 88–97. See Monod, pp. 197–199.

71. Bateson, *Steps to an Ecology of Mind,* p. 315.

72. Like Monod, Bateson, and others.

73. Monod, p. 198.

74. Monod, p. 60.

75. Monod, pp. 60–61.

76. Bateson also prefers to have the evolutionary process begin in living matter. But he faces the problem of a 'mind' that is necessary to explain the 'ecological' responses given by such things as a forest when outside agents are introduced into it. Certain 'differences' demand 'differences' in the overall 'conduct' of the forest if it is to maintain its internal equilibrium and survive. The problem is multiplied when we move from small ecosystems to nature as a whole (*Mind and Nature,* p. 112).

77. Bateson, *Steps,* pp. 3–8.

78. Ibid., p. 8.

79. Monod, p. 118. Other statements by him are grammatically typical in this respect: "Drawn out of the realm of pure chance, the accident enters into that of necessity" (p. 118); "Randomness caught on the wing, preserved, reproduced by the machinery of invariance and thus converted into order . . ." (p. 110). It is noteworthy that he uses passive forms that leave out the subject or agent of the verb. In the last cited passage, as in normal passive usage, it would come after 'by'. But what follows 'by' is a repetition of the *effect,* not a spelling out of the *cause* or agent that uses chance.

80. Monod, p. 60.

81. Bateson, *Steps,* pp. 5–6. The interesting italics are the author's.

82. Negentropy in evolution is defined, so to speak, by Monod as a "mechanism for moving backward in time" (p. 124). Remember that the arrow of time is also that of entropy.

83. Ibid., pp. 119–122.

84. Bateson, *Steps,* pp. 5–6.

85. Bateson defines 'mind' in a much broader sense than that of the human mind. It is a natural or artificial apparatus capable of receiving and processing information. On this 'mind' and its essential characteristics see Bateson, *Steps,* pp. 315 f., 457 f.; *Mind and Nature,* pp. 92 f.

86. Monod, p. 127.

87. Monod, p. 111.

88. Monod, pp. 77 f., pp. 98 f.

89. This seems to be so if we take seriously this statement by Monod: "And since they constitute the *only* possible source of modifications in the genetic text, itself the *sole* repository of the organism's hereditary structure, it necessarily follows that chance *alone* is at the source of every innovation, of all creation in the biosphere. Pure chance, absolutely free but blind, at the very root of the stupendous edifice of evolution; this central concept of modern biology is no longer one among other possible or even conceivable hypotheses. It is today the *sole* conceivable hypothesis, the only one that squares with observed and tested fact. And nothing warrants the supposition—or the hope—that on this score our position is likely ever to be reversed. There is no scientific concept, in any of the sciences, more destructive of anthropocentrism than this one . . ." (pp. 112–113). Then "natural selection" would have to be reduced to 'pure chance', it seems, disregarding the fact that it is largely exercised through the *teleonomy* of the living beings who fight and use each other.

90. Readers might quite fairly and logically ask how I can dare to give the lie to a renowned scientist, who has won a Nobel Prize. My only answer is that I am not attacking him in his specialty, but only insofar as he uses that specialty to make extrapolations in 'natural philosophy'. His own subtitle indicates that: 'An Essay on the Natural Philosophy of Modern Biology'. In that area I cannot help but remark, on the basis of my own specialty, that his 'loose' thinking is too incoherent. In that respect Teilhard is more logical than Monod is.

91. Like Monod, Bateson seems to deny that the two directions are coextensive. For Bateson, negentropy is associated with a *sine qua non*: the existence of 'mental' processes. Then he notes: "Always, however, there is a lower level of division such that the resulting *parts, when considered separately,* lack the complexity necessary to achieve the criteria of mind" (*Mind and Nature,* p. 103; Segundo italics). Bateson explicitly opposes this reflection to Teilhard de Chardin's conception of two vectors of energy (tangential and radial). But there is clearly a misunderstanding here, as the words italicized in Bateson's quote indicate. It is obvious that the parts as isolated entities (as not integrated, *not parts* of) cannot be mental circuits. But why consider them 'separately' when from the beginning we find them forming a circuit, i.e., precisely as *parts*? All that one could logically conclude is that the *whole* inert physical world contains no more than one 'individual' and therefore depends on one single *mind,* whereas each living organism is a mental circuit. But where do we find that one natural 'mind'?

92. Here I should make an important methodological observation first. I am not talking about Jesus' project or the tradition behind it *in exclusive terms.* In other words, I am not claiming to decide *a priori* if other historical projects could or did provide a convergent, complementary, or even superior influence. In line with the objective of this volume, I am simply trying to situate the significance of Jesus of Nazareth within the coordinates of evolution.

93. Properly expressed in this hypothesis, the 'higher' animals are not 'higher' because of the greater and more complex 'order' reigning in them and 'structuring' them. 'Survival' is the chance meeting of 'favorable' genetic anomalies and the chance challenges of the environment. This poses a clear break in continuity to the 'analogy' whereby 'Maxwell's demon', creator of order and negentropy, is seen as a primordial predecessor of the ordering projects of human beings (at least when they take due account of the ecological circuits). Wallace's hypothesis, on the contrary, will maintain the analogy without any break in continuity, as we shall see further on in this chapter. .

94. For the reason noted earlier, Bateson actually begins his study of evolution with life. He presents many convincing reasons for a new epistemology that would deal with the problem of evolution in line with Wallace rather than Darwin. But I think he does not manage to break all the ties that bind him to the epistemology he criticizes, which is hardly surprising. I noted this earlier in citing the conclusion of his first metalogue. We can see it here and there as well as in his thinking, where we find significant omissions, if not clear-cut inconsistencies.

95. It might be noted that the two men kept up an interesting correspondence with each other.

96. Such statements based on historical hindsight are not really 'forecasts' at all. They are designed to convey the decisiveness of certain categories or qualities in the abstract. But it might be added that any explanation like Wallace's would hardly have been practicable, prior to the age of cybernetics and the information industry. It was these two things that introduced the idea of 'mental' in its broader sense into our conception of nature.

97. To avoid falling back into Lamarck's hypothesis, one might well ask how or why those not possessing the 'favorable' genetic anomaly disappear. One would have to say that the same order, balanced with more functions, renders those in need of a variable (a function they do not possess in themselves) more fragile in the face of environmental pressure, even if it is mild. In that case a kind of 'natural selection' functions as an extension of the teleonomy of living beings. I need hardly point out that in this hypothesis the process again appears to be 'mental'. 'Maxwell's demon' again creates order and negentropy by differentiating, not by favoring those most advanced in a given direction.

98. Motoo Kimura, "The Neutral Theory of Molecular Evolution," November 1979, pp. 98–100.

99. Ibid., see the subtitle of the article, p. 98.

100. Evolution is a process, and we know relatively little about how it has developed in *time*. When we compare the 'survival' capacity of zoophytes, who build coral reefs for their habitat, with that of the primates, nothing can convince us that the line running from the former to the latter is constituted by a greater aptitude for survival.

101. See Bateson, *Mind and Nature,* p. 175.

102. See p. 47, above.

103. So observes Teilhard de Chardin. See the citation at the start of section IV of this chapter, p. 61.

104. This is all the more noteworthy since we do see small steps backward, such as the loss of useless functions in changed environments: e.g., the loss of branchial respiration in animals that become terrestrial, the loss of vision in species living in caves without light, and so forth.

105. See Bateson, *Mind and Nature,* p. 103.

106. Bateson, *Steps,* p. 8.

107. Teilhard de Chardin, *The Phenomenon of Man,* p. 244. I say he does not take account of Wallace's hypothesis because he draws that conclusion from the impossibility of classic Darwinism itself. Perhaps somewhat illogically, however, he does not offer another hypothesis in its place: "Life advances by mass effects, by dint of multitudes flung into action without apparent plan. Milliards of germs and millions of adult growths jostling, shoving, and devouring one another. . . . Despite all the waste and ferocity, all the mystery and scandal it involves, there is, as we must be fair and admit, a great deal of biological efficiency in the *struggle for life.* . . . 'Survival of the fittest by

natural selection' is not a meaningless expression, provided it is not taken to imply either a final ideal or a final explanation" (ibid., p. 109).

108. Ibid., p. 263.

109. One example of this extreme: when socialist parties are discredited in a capitalist society because their leaders live bourgeois lives as individuals, and the conclusion is drawn that their political affiliation cannot be sincere.

110. We shall see more clearly in the next chapter why I talk of moral 'reflection' and 'consistency', not of *commandments* or precepts that are to be put into practice on any occasion.

111. See Volume IV, Chapter I. The whole volume is relevant to some extent. There are texts of Vatican II which show the influence of this excessive de-historicization of Jesus of Nazareth based on the way his divinity is conceived. Right after the passage cited earlier (GS:22), without any break, the conciliar text goes on to say: "An innocent lamb, he merited life for us by the free shedding of his own blood. In him God reconciled us to Himself and among ourselves. He delivered us from enslavement to the devil and sin, so that each one of us can say with the Apostle: The Son of God 'loved me and gave himself up for me' (Gal 2:20)" (GS:22). In this passage the real-life history of Jesus and the reasons for his life and death seem to have been overlooked or forgotten completely.

112. It is interesting to note that the Spanish translation of this text changes the order of the official Latin text in a classic theological locus. It writes of Jesus as *'hombre perfecto',* when the theological tradition of the first ecumenical councils indicates we should say *'perfecto hombre',* which is obviously not the same thing.

113. Otherwise my following remarks might occasion the tenacious misunderstanding I have been combatting since Volume I: i.e., that Jesus can be meaningful only for the 'religious' human being, that he automatically ceases to be so for the atheist.

Chapter III: The Primordial from the Standpoint of Jesus

114. See the beginnings of a new response, more ontological (both Heideggerian and scholastic) than evolutionary, in Karl Rahner's article on 'The Theological Concept of Concupiscentia'.

115. Note the close linguistic relationship between 'prince' and 'principle'.

116. See Rudolf Bultmann, *Theology of the New Testament,* I, pp. 187 and 164–183.

117. Ibid., p. 228.

118. Bateson, *Mind and Nature,* pp. 58–59.

119. Ibid., p. 58.

120. Ibid., p. 59.

121. Ibid.

122. Ibid., pp. 126–128.

123. Deactivations that are desperate in a certain sense, that are looking for an 'energy' youthfulness that has been lost forever because it has been emptied into a circuit entailing 'time', which means 'age'.

124. In this connection see Bateson's interesting memorandum to the Regents of the University of California about flexibility and obsolescence in educational methods. It is an Appendix in *Mind and Nature,* pp. 215 f.

125. Buchsbaum comment cited by E. F. Schumacher in *Small Is Beautiful.* See Chapter I, pp. 38–39 in this volume, and note 61.

126. Bateson, *Mind and Nature,* p. 127. His numerals refer to principles that he has already set forth and that he summarizes here.

127. Ibid.

128. Just as somatic changes achieved by 'mental' mechanisms do not communicate with the genetic code. That would be the end of evolution.

129. S. Freud, *Civilization and Its Discontents.* I choose this work even though I know it represents only one stage in his thinking, and even granting that, that there is no firm consensus as to how his deepest thought is to be interpreted. I am also leaving aside Freud's *general* criticisms of religion (see, e.g., *The Future of an Illusion*). Here I focus solely on his treatment of the Christian maxim in the Sermon on the Mount, even though it and other such maxims may go back to earlier stages of the Jewish religion.

130. Freud, *Civilization and Its Discontents,* p. 53.

131. "Since a man does not have unlimited quantities of psychical energy at his disposal" (ibid., p. 56).

132. Ibid., p. 73.

133. See Bateson's critique in the metalogue entitled: "What Is an Instinct?" (*Steps to an Ecology of Mind,* pp. 38–58).

134. Freud, *Civilization and Its Discontents,* pp. 61–62.

135. Ibid., p. 56.

136. Ibid., pp. 57–58. "By turning away from its sexual aims and transforming the instinct into an impulse with an *inhibited aim*" (ibid., p. 54).

137. Ibid., p. 59.

138. Ibid., p. 62.

139. Ibid., p. 63.

140. Ibid., pp. 64–65.

141. Another important issue will come up later. But it is appropriate right here to point out that two things run counter to the coherence of Freud's thinking about culture. First, it follows from what he has already written, as cited here, that the lack of supporting psychical energy would render totally ineffective (hence innocuous) the Christian precept as a former of culture, because it runs counter to both the erotic impulses and the aggressive instincts. Second, the real cultural progress in both quantity and complexity, which is noted by Freud, proves that the dissatisfaction generated by culture does not consist of the 'normal' sexual repression imposed by culture. It is due to the fact that society, while imposing that repression, does not succeed in achieving the 'sublimated' ideals which it has promised, and which human beings continue to regard as more important than the repression, *in principle*. Thus, as Marcuse claims, cultural discontent is due to the degree of repression actually exercised, to the 'surplus repression' which one seeks to justify with that principle. In short, it is due to an unnecessary and inhuman degree of repression.

142. Freud, *Civilization and Its Discontents,* p. 64.

143. "It is always possible to bind together a considerable number of people in love, so long as there are other people left over to receive the manifestations of their aggressiveness" (ibid., p. 68).

144. Ibid., p. 47.

145. Ibid., pp. 73 f.

146. That Freud practically equates the death instinct with the direction of entropy is obvious from his first treatment of it in *Civilization and Its Discontents* (p. 73), where he describes it as a force "seeking to dissolve those units and to bring them back to their primaeval, inorganic state." Marcuse picks up this hypothesis and summarizes it when he describes the death instinct as a 'quest for Nirvana' or even a 'Nirvana principle' (Marcuse, *Eros and Civilization,* p. 98).

147. See Freud, *Civilization and Its Discontents,* p. 73 and *passim.* But this direction against self, which comes from aggressiveness, puts an end to the explanation given for the origin of the latter: self-preservation (see ibid., pp. 64 f.). That is why I think the hypothesis offered here is more consistent and authentically Freudian.

148. This is the hypothesis developed very ably by Erich Fromm in *Escape from Freedom,* especially in Chapter V: 'Mechanisms of Escape'. There Fromm analyzes authoritarianism (sadomasochism), destructiveness, and automatic conformity (pp. 157–230).

149. This makes clear how right Marcuse was in pointing up an almost insuperable mistake of theological language and culture: "The notion that Eros and Agape may after all be one and the same—not that Eros is Agape but that Agape is Eros—may sound strange after almost two thousand years of theology" (*Eros and Civilization,* p. 192).

150. Charles Péguy, *Le Mystère de la charité de Jeanne d'Arc.*

151. Charles Péguy, *Le Mystère des Saints Innocents.*

152. Remember that Paul himself indicated his opposition in principle to any and all discrimination based on sex, religion, or social class, although he did not fight directly against it in reality.

153. I touched on that tendency in Volume I (*Faith and Ideologies*), Chapter V, section I, pp. 120 f.

154. Failing to realize this circuit relationship, people are stuck in the linear conception of evolution expounded by Darwin, which denies purpose and adopts Spencer's expression, 'survival of the fittest' as an apt description of the mechanism of evolution. As we saw, Wallace's conception was different. And Teilhard de Chardin did manage to correct the Darwinian view somewhat insofar as he came closer to circuit logic. See Chapter 2, section IV, p. 61 in this volume.

155. One more example under the general theme of legal rights may show us even more clearly that those rights cannot assert themselves simply by the expansion of the model; that they depend on an egalitarian *circuit,* which in reality does not exist, if they are not to prove contradictory and counterproductive. Consider the undeniable right of the female to be treated on a footing of equality with the male. Linear logic assumes that this liberation of the woman, inscribed in legal rights in those countries we might consider 'the fittest', would then spread like an oil slick to the other countries of the world. But the logic involved is really much more complicated. Female equality with the male can become a legal 'right' only in those countries that can pay the price it entails. It will be accepted democratically only if it does not lower the proportion of male benefits and assets to raise those of the female. So a country already consuming forty percent of the assets of the planet will consume an even greater percentage, with consequent crises (circuit deactivations) in the poorest countries. As anyone can see by merely looking at the latter countries, every economic crisis brings with it—besides other even more basic violations, of course—a further reduction in income-producing labor. That translates into a further step backward for the whole issue of female equality.

156. Declaration of the Brazilian Episcopal Conference, October 21, 1976, in a pastoral letter of its representative commission.

157. To be sure, accepting this ploy indicates a curious forgetfulness of the *means* used by Christendom, when it was able to use them, to extend and defend faith in Jesus.

158. By placing Jesus above and beyond all conflicts and ideological camps, these christologies ensure that his death seems to be totally disconnected with his own life and activity.

159. This connection or relationship is accepted by christologies insofar as the death of the redeemer is viewed as a punishment by God for the sins of human beings. Thus, in his 'sacrifice', Jesus supposedly took those sins upon himself, though in an *extrinsic* way.

160. Guerrero (*El otro Jesús*) maintains a sort of divinization in the life of Jesus. Not surprisingly, then, he takes for granted that Jesus' last words were those of the finishing touches in Luke: "Father, into your hands I commend my spirit" (Lk 23:46). But one should not ignore or be unaware of the characteristic redactional work of the third evangelist, much less the necessary distinction between prepaschal and postpaschal understanding of Jesus.

161. In very different categories, which he himself calls 'scholastic', Karl Rahner introduces us to this whole problem in his essay on 'The Theological Concept of Concupiscentia'. Note that his references in the article to 'flesh' and 'law of the members' indicate that Romans 7:14–25 is being taken into consideration. At one point he writes: "In reality of course the whole 'nature' given prior to freedom offers resistance to the 'person's' free and total disposition of himself, so that the boundary between 'person' and 'nature' stands as it were vertically in regard to the horizontal line which divides spirituality from sensibility in man. . . . Now as we have just shown, the spontaneous act of desire, arising from the bare dynamism of nature and directed to a wittingly apprehended object, is one of the metaphysically necessary presuppositions of a concrete free decision made by a finite subject" (*Theological Investigations* I, pp. 364–65). If that is true then the 'firstborn of all creatures' or finite beings, Jesus, could not escape that metaphysical law if he is to be a fully human being. That is clearly suggested by Rahner himself near the end of his article. Writing about concupiscence, the equivalent of Paul's 'law of the members', he notes: "It is also the form in which the Christian experiences *Christ's* sufferings . . ." (ibid., p. 382; my italics).

162. Luke informs us that Jesus 'learned', moved from ignorance and error to truth, in the most 'theological' part of his Gospel (2:52). In Volume II, p. 57, I noted the peculiarly theological cast of the literary genre embodied in the 'infancy narratives' of Matthew and Luke. See also Hebrews 5:8.

163. Jesus, perfectly and completely human being, had to go through the 'social' law *par excellence* in his person and his project. As Bateson would put it, he had to lose his own 'autonomy' and that of his project (*Mind and Nature*, pp. 126 f.) so that they might continue.

164. On this topic see my book, *The Liberation of Theology*, Chapter 6, pp. 162 f.

165. See the Introduction and Chapter 1 of Volume IV in this series: *The Christ of the Ignatian Exercises*.

166. The scandal obviously does not come from the exegesis or simple reading of the gospel message. It comes from the danger of a symbiosis of Christianity and Marxism that promotes social change by fomenting the class struggle until it breaks out openly. Today no one dares to expurgate the *text* of the Gospels, as Marcion did in his day. Now it is much easier to forget or overlook a good portion of their clearest and most immediate content.

167. See Luke 6:20 and Luke 6:27. See also Volume II (*The Historical Jesus of the Synoptics*), Chapter 7, section II.

168. There is not the slightest variant in the manuscripts, nor the slightest doubt about the only meaning of the Greek conjunction *hina* ('so that') here. Translations of the Biblical text have no right to water down Mark in order to bring its text in line with that

of Matthew, giving us *'thus . . . unless'* instead of 'so that . . . lest'. Yet that is precisely what the *Nueva Biblia Española* does.

169. The Greek word used in Matthew 16:4 and 21:17 has this connotation of 'stalking off' and is correctly translated by the *Nueva Biblia Española* as *los dejó plantados*. Jesus obviously shows *impatience* with the bad faith of his adversaries.

170. One need hardly allude to the many insulting terms that Jesus employs in Matthew alone: idolaters, adulterers, renegades, brood of vipers, blind fools, hypocrites, and so forth. Note that these evaluations point to the inner heart, which would seem to contradict the precept of Matthew 7:1.

171. Note the *Conclusiones finales* of the Puebla Conference: "Every ideology is partial, since no particular group can claim to identify its aspirations with society as a whole. Thus an ideology will be legitimate if the interests it defends are legitimate, and if it respects the fundamental rights of the other groups in a nation. In this positive sense, ideologies seem to be necessary for social activity insofar as they are mediations for action" (n. 535). The Conference assumes that an impartial kind of thinking does exist: "Neither the gospel message nor the doctrine or social teaching deriving from it are ideologies" (n. 540). Sticking solely to the gospel message, we might very well ask whether staying outside the ideological realm derives from the 'neutrality' or impartiality of Jesus himself.

Chapter IV: Jesus and the Recapitulation of the Universe

172. By 'closer' here I mean a kind of thinking which, even though it makes use of transcendent data that cannot possibly be verified by ordinary experience, does try to be consistent with itself and with the methods used successfully by cognition in those investigations where experience is the criterion of verification in one way or another.

173. Marx's case is a bit different, at least in the order followed. Marx began with a critique of the prevailing epistemology. Then, in later life, he tried to show how his new epistemology scientifically opened the way for practical and theoretical discoveries. Thus, although both psychoanalysis and historical materialism have had difficulties in winning scientific status, there is no doubt that the former would fall more readily into the category of science if we were to draw a dividing line between science and ideology.

174. Teilhard moved from his scientific discoveries in paleontology to what he claimed was a new epistemology, but he did not manage to formulate the latter in a critical way. This explains, I think, why many scientists minimize his value on the one hand, while a wave of 'enthusiasm' broke over him, and weighed him down, on the other.

175. Teilhard de Chardin, *The Phenomenon of Man,* pp. 34–35.

176. Ibid., p. 36.

177. Ibid., p. 52. Translator's note: 'the figure' is used here instead of 'our picture' in the English translation of the book since it fits in better with Segundo's employment of the phrase later and is an accurate transliteration of the text.

178. Or 'self-justifying' if you prefer. In other words, they do not depend for their validity on what the human being perceives as external. To a large extent they are imposed on that as prefabricated molds or "patterns" (see Bateson, *Steps to an Ecology of Mind,* p. 314).

179. Monod, *Chance and Necessity,* p. 176.

180. Ibid.

181. See note 50, above, for Monod's understanding of the term 'animism'.

182. Monod, *Chance and Necessity,* p. 172.

183. As I noted before, it is not easy to pinpoint Bateson's thinking on the matter. All the epistemological elements in his work point in the direction that is the opposite of Monod's: e.g., universal analogy, loose thinking (to be combined with strict or objective thinking), his conception of nature as 'mental', etc. Nevertheless some of his explicit statements and positions are hard to fit into that framework. As we saw, for example, he concludes in his first metalogue in *Steps* that 'things will always go toward muddle and mixedness' (p. 8). And as we shall see in this chapter, he seems to reject the idea of any overcoming of death, at least at the level of the individual.

184. Not forgetting, however, that this 'phenomenon' already contains *transcendent* data, logical extrapolations that go beyond what any empirical 'seeing' can verify.

185. See Teilhard de Chardin, *The Phenomenon of Man,* pp. 65–66. Criticisms from the theological quarter, such as the one that Teilhard did not take due account of something as radical as sin and its force, could be due to this hasty rush from the ideal to its fulfillment. But I think their source is probably nothing more than a misunderstanding.

186. As I see it, the term 'radial energy' is practically equivalent to negentropy in Teilhard's terminology, since progressive complexity, centration, and consciousness are attributed to it.

187. Teilhard de Chardin, *The Phenomenon of Man,* p. 66.

188. Moreover, this 'linear' rush toward Omega leads Teilhard de Chardin to implicit conclusions of a theological, sociological, and political nature. Thus he assumes that the growing population of the planet and its progressive, inevitable interdependence will lead human beings to love each other more (see "The Ultimate Earth" in *The Phenomenon of Man,* pp. 273 f.).

189. When the reader heard Monod saying that the universe is 'deaf' to the music of the human being, this eloquent passage may have reminded him or her of Proust's talk about the musical 'hostages' that make definitive death less likely (see Volume II of this series, Appendix I, section II).

190. According to Bateson, the world of mental process is "a slowly self-healing tautology" (*Mind and Nature,* p. 206).

191. "However good the man, he becomes a toxic substance if he stays around too long" (ibid., p. 208).

192. Ibid., p. 126.

193. I am leaving aside the fact that Bateson's argument is used to justify a very minority kind of death. He is talking about one where a person has created meaning in life and then gives in to the temptation to cling to his or her autonomy rather than giving that meaning the new possibilities that other human beings might have by using the same elements over again. That is the sort of death Rilke describes as issuing from a life in which there was love, caring, and a meaning. But what are we to say of the vast majority of lives that arrive at death after nothing but a desperate struggle for mere survival, insofar as we can see?

194. Bateson, *Mind and Nature,* pp. 150, 175.

195. This is obviously true for sexuality and the human couple. It is completely unrealistic and futile to view it as a functional component of the species. The energy that dynamizes sex relations *can* go as far as a concern for the species, but it is born of a need of the individual. It is not without reason that a rigid brand of Marxism has regarded Freud and psychoanalysis as enemies, being forced at the same time to sacrifice a promised sexual liberation for the sake of societal welfare.

196. The choice of art is not arbitrary. Bateson points out that the technical world often destroys meaning with its escalade of 'interests'. As corrective factors, he points to those intimately bound up with meaning: art (*Steps,* pp. 446–447); religion (ibid., p. 144); dreams and poetry (ibid., pp. 446–447); and so forth.

197. Teilhard de Chardin, *Christianisme et évolution,* unpublished text of 1945. For another English version see Rideau, *The Thought of Teilhard de Chardin,* p. 508.

198. I find this hint in an important observation by Bateson regarding the 'original' sense of religion before it degenerates into magic or whatever: "I do not believe that the original purpose of the rain dance was to make 'it' rain. I suspect that this is a degenerate misunderstanding of a much more profound religious need: to affirm membership in what we may call the *ecological tautology . . .*" (*Mind and Nature,* p. 209).

199. See Volume III (*The Humanist Christology of Paul*), Chapter 8.

200. It is worth noting that the text says that nothing 'profane' will enter on the one hand, but that 'the wealth of the nations' will enter. The latter could be regarded as very 'profane' indeed, since 'the nations' is a technical term for the pagan peoples. Of course exegesis could interpret this as a spoliation of those 'nations' in favor of Jerusalem (which would not be an indication of true universality, as in Isaiah 60:3–11). But it remains significant that in this iconic language the new earth, the heavenly Jerusalem, prolongs and takes in terrestrial values.

201. Explicitly in 1 Corinthians 15:36 f. It also appears more indirectly in the 'new life' that the members of the communities known to Paul lead, although with relapses (see Rom 6:20 f. and *passim*).

202. In *Gaudium et spes* Vatican II speaks of the resurrection in a new way: "Then, with death defeated, the children of God will be resurrected in Christ. What was sown in weakness and corruption will be clothed with incorruptibility. While love and its works will perdure, all creatures . . . will be freed from bondage to uselessness. . . . The values of human dignity, brotherhood, and freedom, and indeed all the excellent fruits of nature and our effort, after having propagated them on earth, we will find them again, purified of every stain, burnished, and transfigured" (GS:39). Note that the *newness* of this statement is based completely on Pauline texts that had been overlooked, not used, or minimized by exegesis.

203. See the citation from Monod in section I of this chapter, pp. 95–96.

204. Another important and innovative statement of Vatican II (GS:22).

205. In *The Phenomenon of Man,* Teilhard de Chardin writes, for example, that "Christian love is incomprehensible to those who have not experienced it" (p. 295). Even more clearly in this vein is the following statement about the 'Christian' phylum: "Reset in an evolution interpreted as an ascent of consciousness, this phylum, in its trend towards a synthesis based on love, progresses precisely in the direction presumed for the *leading-shoot* of biogenesis" (ibid., p. 298).

Chapter V: By Way of Conclusion

206. I know from personal experience that people continue to preach a Jesus for individual morality or, at best, an idealistic Jesus, in the centers of world power that are closest to the responsibilities engendered by this problematic.

207. I need hardly warn my readers at length against the mistake of confusing or equating 'evolution' with 'developmentalism', reformism, linear progress, or any other kind of non-dialectical thinking. Although so-called 'evolutionism' may have been

presented thus at the beginning, I feel the previous chapters make it clear that such is not my view of the matter and also indicate why it is not.

208. As I indicated earlier, I am surprised by the lack of logical rigor in Monod's thinking when he tries to move from his own scientific specialty to the realm of epistemology. Readers should remember that 'loose' thinking is opposed to 'precise' or 'strict' thinking, not to thinking done rigorously and logically. And rigor in one field does not ensure it in another field—with all due respect to Monod as a winner of the Nobel Prize.

209. All the more since the necessary (to what extent?) exclusion of anthropomorphisms, of *purpose* in particular, makes it all the more difficult to apply those categories to the area of human planning.

210. In any case, there is importance in the fact that for centuries the Christian institution did not show any serious or major concern, as the Pauline communities did, in getting those 'weak in the faith' to move toward an adult, mature Christian faith. Moreover, for reasons of survival, it abstained from labelling pre-Christian attitudes of a mass nature as 'weakness of faith'. Consider, for example, the conception of history as a 'vale of tears' where we live as 'exiles', and where we are being tested by the criterion of the Law.

211. My readers would do well to go back to those conclusions in Chapter 9 of Volume III (*The Humanist Christology of Paul*). Obviously those conclusions from Paul's christological efforts were already influenced by the 'context' from which I was making my analysis. It could not be otherwise. I am not suggesting that Paul himself drew those conclusions clearly and explicitly, but neither did I invent them. The internal logic and coherence of Paul's own thought led me to draw those conclusions, even when Paul himself did not. Readers may judge for themselves whether this is true or not by examining my further reflections in this chapter.

212. This display of divine power may have managed to win pardon for those human beings who took refuge in divine mercy; but it left intact the human being's inclination to Sin and its alienation by the latter, as experience makes clear enough.

213. This is quite aside from other important elements I mentioned in Volume III. One of crucial importance is the dialectical gradation of the three stages of humanity pointed out by Paul. In this connection one thing should be remembered. Despite his chronological priority, Adam in Paradise is situated by Paul in the *second* stage since he is in a certain sense *under the Law* (see Rom 5:13), whereas one who follows Christ has been liberated from it (see Rom 6:15; 7:6; Gal 3:23–26).

214. Not in vain has tradition intoned 'O happy Fault' in this connection. But we must also avoid going to the other extreme, which is equally out of tune with an evolutionary perspective: i.e., regarding the sin of Adam as a necessary step from the infantile human stage to true human maturity. That would be an even greater mistake, at least insofar as Paul's anthropology is concerned.

215. Thus sheer logic indicates that it would not make sense for Paul to picture a *complete* creation *first* (before Adam's sin). That would run counter to his view of what God thinks, wills, and hopes for the human being: i.e., his view of the reason for the creation of humanity.

216. Only when we assume this transcendent datum does faith become a crucial factor in the free working of the human being rather than a substitute for such work before the judgment of God.

217. As I have said before, transcendent data always take shape by leading thought reasonably, and in the direction suggested by experience, beyond what the latter can

verify. The element of anthropological faith in these data is the fact that we cannot verify to what extent our reasonings remain valid after being extrapolated, except through witnesses.

218. As I have noted, the philosophy held by Teilhard de Chardin bent him in this direction. It is undoubtedly one of the weakest points in his thinking.

219. The most that can be verified is that every human being acts *as if* it were free. Science cannot determine whether its decisions are predetermined by nature, the cunning of reason, or God. Such questions are not proper for science. They fall within the domain of philosophy or theology (insofar as it explicitates the content of spiritual traditions), both on the level of technical, specialized study and that of common sense.

220. Statements by Dom Ivo Lorscheider, as reported by the newspaper *Zero Hora* of Porto Alegre (July 5, 1981), p. 39. The italics are mine.

221. I think Machoveč comes close to making this discovery in some of the sections of his work that I cited in Chapter V of Volume I (*Faith and Ideologies*): i.e., where he writes about the resurrection of Jesus and the absence of the pristine values of socialism in those societies where socialism has been turned into a reality. But I say he 'comes close' because he seems to retreat quickly to problems of an individual cast. Those problems are real enough, but they unduly circumscribe the 'political' relevance of the theme of *resurrection*.

222. This conception also transforms thinking about eschatology in a radical way. In Volume III, we saw this in the case of Paul, particularly in Romans 5 and Romans 8.

223. Infantile because it is precisely the opposite logic that is applied to all the working hypotheses of science. If chance were the most 'economical' explanation of any type of 'order', then science as a whole would cease to function. We can, of course, acknowledge the primacy of teleonomy but assume that it is a characteristic of our minds rather than of things in themselves. That doesn't really change much, however, because we have no access to things except our mind thus structured. In the last analysis, the latter is what guides us in our actions.

224. See the text of Leonardo Boff cited in Chapter 1 of Volume II (*The Historical Jesus of the Synoptics*), on preaching the cross (and resurrection) of Jesus Christ today and what it means.

225. Mario Benedetti, "Victoria del vencido," in the anthology of his works entitled *Letras de emergencia,* pp. 131–132. I need not remind my readers of good will that the remarks hold true for all 'just' causes, and even for those regarded as such in the hearts of their adherents although others may judge them mistaken.

Reference Bibliography

1. Works Cited by Abbreviations

DS. Denzinger, Bannwart, and Schoenmetzer. *Enchiridion Symbolorum.* Segundo cites the Spanish edition: *El magisterio de la Iglesia,* Barcelona: Herder, 1955.

GS. *Gaudium et spes.* Vatican II, Pastoral Constitution on the Church in the Modern World, December 7, 1965.

2. Works Cited by Title

Nueva Biblia Española. Edición Latinoamericana. Spanish translation edited by L. A. Schoekel and J. Mateos, Madrid: Ed. Cristiandad, 1976.

3. Works Cited by Author

Bateson, G. *Mind and Nature: A Necessary Unity.* New York: E. P. Dutton, 1979.

Bateson, G. *Steps to an Ecology of Mind.* New York: Ballantine Books, 1972.

Benedetti, M. *Letras de emergencia.* Mexico City: Ed. Nueva Imagen, 1980.

Buchsbaum, Ralph and Mildred. *Basic Ecology.* Pittsburgh: Boxwood Press, 1957.

Bultmann, R. *Theology of the New Testament.* Eng. trans., New York: Scribner's, 1951 and 1955. Two volumes.

Cox, H. *The Secular City.* Revised edition. New York: Macmillan, 1966.

Eagleson and Scharper (eds.). *Puebla and Beyond: Documentation and Commentary.* Maryknoll, NY: Orbis Books, 1979.

Freud, S. *Civilization and Its Discontents.* Eng. trans., New York: W. W. Norton, 1962.

Freud, S. *The Future of an Illusion.* Eng. trans., New York: W. W. Norton, 1961.

Fromm, E. *Escape from Freedom.* New York: Avon Books/Discus, 1965.

Gadamer, H. G. *Truth and Method.* Eng. trans., New York: Seabury Press, 1975.

Gibellini, R. (ed.). *Frontiers of Theology in Latin America.* Eng. trans., Maryknoll, NY: Orbis Books, 1978.

Guerrero, J. R. *El otro Jesús.* Salamanca: Ed. Sígueme, 1976.

Heidegger, M. *Being and Time.* Eng. trans., New York: Harper & Row, 1962.

Hofstadter, D. R. "Meta-magical Themes," *Scientific American,* May 1981.

Hunneus, F. "Una función científico-cultural del concepto de Gestalt," *Acta psic. Latin. Am.,* 1976, 22:88–97.

Huxley, J. *Evolution in Action.* New York: Penguin Books, 1963.

Kimura, M. "The Neutral Theory of Molecular Evolution," *Scientific American,* November 1979, pp. 98–100.

Küng, H. *On Being A Christian.* Eng. trans., Garden City, NY: Doubleday, 1976.

Machoveč, M. *A Marxist Looks at Jesus*. Eng. trans., Philadelphia: Fortress Press, 1976.

Marcuse, H. *Eros and Civilization*. Boston: Beacon Press, 1974.

Marx, K. *Capital*. Volume One. Eng. trans., New York: Vintage Books, 1977.

Monod, J. *Chance and Necessity*. Eng. trans., New York: Vintage Books, 1972.

Péguy, C. *Le Mystère de la charité de Jeanne d'Arc*. 1910.

Péguy, C. *Le Mystère des Saints Innocents*. 1912.

Rahner, K. "Current Problems in Christology," *Theological Investigations I*. Baltimore: Helicon Press, 1961, pp. 149–200.

Rahner, K. "The Theological Concept of Concupiscentia," *Theological Investigations I*. Baltimore: Helicon Press, 1961, pp. 347–382.

Rahner, K. and Overhage, P. *El problema de la hominización: Sobre el origen biológico del hombre*. Spanish trans., Madrid: Ed. Cristiandad, 1973.

Rideau, E. *The Thought of Teilhard de Chardin*. Eng. trans., New York: Harper & Row, 1967.

Schumacher, E. F. *Small Is Beautiful: Economics As If People Mattered*. New York: Harper & Row/Perennial Library, 1973.

Segundo, J. L. "Capitalism Versus Socialism: Crux Theologica," Chapter 11 in Gibellini (see above).

Segundo, J. L. *The Christ of the Ignatian Exercises*. Volume IV of Jesus of Nazareth Yesterday and Today. Eng. trans., Maryknoll, NY: Orbis Books, 1987.

Segundo, J. L. *The Community Called Church*. Volume 1 of A Theology For Artisans of a New Humanity. Eng. trans., Maryknoll, NY: Orbis Books, 1973.

Segundo, J. L. "Conversión y reconciliación en la teología de la liberación," *Perspectiva Teológica*, 7, 1975, pp. 164–178. Spanish summary in *Selecciones de Teología*, 15, 1976, pp. 263–275.

Segundo, J. L. *Faith and Ideologies*. Volume I of Jesus of Nazareth Yesterday and Today. Eng. trans., Maryknoll, NY: Orbis Books, 1984.

Segundo, J. L. *Grace and the Human Condition*. Volume 2 of A Theology For Artisans of a New Humanity. Eng. trans., Maryknoll, NY: Orbis Books, 1973.

Segundo, J. L. *The Hidden Motives of Pastoral Action*. Eng. trans., Maryknoll, NY: Orbis Books, 1977.

Segundo, J. L. *The Historical Jesus of the Synoptics*. Volume II of Jesus of Nazareth Yesterday and Today. Eng. trans., Maryknoll, NY: Orbis Books, 1985.

Segundo, J. L. *The Humanist Christology of Paul*. Volume III of Jesus of Nazareth Yesterday and Today. Eng. trans., Maryknoll, NY: Orbis Books, 1986.

Segundo, J. L. *The Liberation of Theology*. Eng. trans., Maryknoll, NY: Orbis Books, 1976.

Stace, W. T. *Religion and the Modern Mind*. Philadelphia: Lippincott, 1952.

Teilhard de Chardin, P. *L'activation de l'énergie*. Paris: Ed. du Seuil, 1963. Eng. trans., *The Activation of Energy*. New York: Harcourt Brace Jovanovich, 1971.

Teilhard de Chardin, P. *The Divine Milieu*. Eng. trans., New York: Harper & Row, 1960.

Teilhard de Chardin, P. *The Phenomenon of Man*. Eng. trans., New York: Harper & Row/Torchbooks, 1961.

General Index

145